Cinematic Mythmaking

Books by Irving Singer

Cinematic Mythmaking: Philosophy in Film

Philosophy of Love: A Partial Summing-Up

Ingmar Bergman, Cinematic Philosopher: Reflections on His Creativity

Three Philosophical Filmmakers: Hitchcock, Welles, Renoir

Reality Transformed: Film as Meaning and Technique

Sex: A Philosophical Primer, expanded edition

Feeling and Imagination: The Vibrant Flux of Our Existence

Explorations in Love and Sex

Sex: A Philosophical Primer

George Santayana, Literary Philosopher

*Meaning in Life:**
The Creation of Value
The Pursuit of Love
The Harmony of Nature and Spirit

*The Nature of Love:**
Plato to Luther
Courtly and Romantic
The Modern World

*Mozart and Beethoven: The Concept of Love in Their Operas**

The Goals of Human Sexuality

Santayana's Aesthetics

Essays in Literary Criticism by George Santayana (editor)

The Nature and Pursuit of Love: The Philosophy of Irving Singer
(ed. David Goicoechea)

(*indicates reprints with new author's preface for each volume, available via the MIT Press Irving Singer Library)

Cinematic Mythmaking

Philosophy in Film

Irving Singer

The MIT Press
Cambridge, Massachusetts
London, England

First MIT Press paperback edition, 2010

MIT Press books may be purchased at special quantity discounts for business or sales promotional use. For information, please e-mail special_sales@mitpress.mit.edu or write to Special Sales Department, The MIT Press, 55 Hayward Street, Cambridge, MA 02142.

This book was set in Palatino by Graphic Composition, Inc. and was printed and bound in the United States of America.

Library of Congress Cataloging-in-Publication Data

Singer, Irving.
Cinematic mythmaking : philosophy in film / Irving Singer.
p. cm.
Includes bibliographical references and index.
ISBN 978-0-262-19589-8 (hardcover : alk. paper)—978-0-262-51515-3 (pb. : alk. paper) 1. Myth in motion pictures.
I. Title.
PN1995.9.M96S56 2008
791.43'615—dc22
2008017023

10 9 8 7 6 5 4 3 2

To Naomi Mae, Future Cinephile

Contents

Prefatory Note ix

Introduction: Philosophical Dimensions of Myth and Cinema 1

1 *The Lady Eve* 13

2 Pygmalion Variations 53

3 *The Heiress* and *Washington Square* 83

4 Cocteau: The Mythological Poetry of Film 139

5 Mythmaking in Kubrick and Fellini 195

Notes 231

Index 239

Prefatory Note

This book is the accumulation of thoughts and writings that resulted from years during which I taught film courses at MIT that were jointly listed in the philosophy section as well as programs in literature and comparative media studies. The work reflects my attempt to probe levels of meaning that film critics often neglect and film analysts sometimes subordinate to the study of technical details. The exploration that I present ranges from a screwball comedy of the early forties to dramatic films of another sort in the last years before the twenty-first century began. Because my mission is not historical, I feel justified in letting the chapters stand alone without much attempt to link them in any causal or temporal pattern. The introduction defines their overall intention, to which I need add only one general remark in advance: Since all of my literary efforts emanate directly from my personal experience, and since that changes in the course of time and individual development, I find that ending each particular book leaves me with the feeling that it would have been very different, and possibly better, if I were now to begin it anew. There is no definitive termination in this text, or in anything else I write. In the present case, neither is there a concluding chapter, since I believe that future explorations of a similar sort may be forthcoming.

From the reader's viewpoint, my mode of writing has an advantage inasmuch as it precludes the pomposity of authorial claims to objective assurance. I merely offer a panoply of insights and ideas that matter to me and issue out of my response as a devoted, somewhat trained, spectator. I invite those who join me in this enterprise to savor their own experience as fellow members of the audience, whatever that experience may be and however much it contrasts with mine. If I fail to induce this mutually enjoyable communication between us, my remarks will have been largely wasted. Not entirely, however, since the making of them was, for me at least, both life-enhancing and a great deal of fun.

The book is dedicated to my granddaughter Naomi Mae Singer in the hope that someday she will love motion pictures as much as I do. I am grateful to her for that incentive, and to friends—some of whose names appear in the notes—who have generously given me help and encouragement throughout the many drafts of composition.

I. S.

Introduction: Philosophical Dimensions of Myth and Cinema

In earlier books I argued that the aesthetic value in cinematic art is a function of both the meanings and the techniques that filmmakers employ for the sake of communication to a receptive audience. In addition I drew upon my general belief that through their meaningfulness, as presented by relevant techniques, many films are capable of having what I called "philosophical" scope related to the problem solving of philosophy proper but in no way reducible to it.

As illustration of my perspective, I analyzed several noteworthy films, briefly or at some length. In this book I follow a slightly different procedure. I explore the hidden as well as overt use, in various films, of major myths that structure and pervade the affective and cognitive lives that people have led in the past and in the present. I formerly thought I would call the book *Film as Mythmaking*, without any further specification in a subtitle, and what that suggests still remains as a principal theme in my chapters. But I now perceive that the actual approach in this work is more comprehensive. It is also a study of philosophical elements that contribute to the visual, literary, and sonic effects within the aesthetic contents of the films I discuss. In some respects the mythic is central, but not exclusively.

Having made this qualification, I can nevertheless begin by considering what the nature of myth may be, and how it performs a crucial role in cinematic art and even philosophy itself. In the history of human civilization, myths often had a religious origin. They served to explain how the gods and goddesses of antiquity or primitive society entered into the affairs of mortals, frequently emblazoning moral goals that ordinary men and women pursued in daily life. The myths of creation sought to reveal how the entire cosmos, or at least a major part of it, came into being; the myths of hero worship celebrated the extraordinary feats of chosen individuals who provided a link to the divine source of everything; the ideational myths focused upon the valuational aspects of feeling and behavior ascribed to either the deities or the heroic protagonists in one or another myth. Very often all three types of myth were interwoven as mutually fortifying strands that articulated in their unity a sense of reality that emanated from a particular society. This construction took the shape of communal narratives whose fictional as well as nonfictional inventiveness could awaken the imagination of anyone who loves a good story. Myths are therefore works of art that purvey a significant level of insight about the world and our concrete involvement in it.

A kindred effort is refined and codified in the abstract investigations that belong to what we call "philosophy." Instead of fabricating intriguing tales, philosophers address issues that often resemble their cognate themes in the mythic traditions but are formulated within a framework of rationality that relies on methods of logic and partly scientific sophistication. While myths may enter into a philosopher's writing, as they do most magnificently throughout the Platonic dialogues, they normally function as illumination subsidiary to detailed argumentation rather than as evocative storytelling. An underlying worldview that permeates some work in philosophy may itself be deemed a mythological perspective. Even so, however, the investigation being done above ground, so to speak, must justify itself as a cognitive procedure of an alternate type. In art the situation is reversed. The fictive intent is evident and the philosophical substrata remain hidden within some intricate texture, often mythological, that generally incorporates them without our being aware of their operative presence prior to an aesthetic analysis that brings them to the surface.

What I do in this book, as in my others on the nature of film, mainly pertains to the latter effort. I am not a historian of either local or world mythologies, nor am I a film theorist who studies the technical wonders that enable a movie to attain its unique mode of communication. I am interested in myths as components in the meaningfulness conveyed through cinematic techniques and therefore pertinent to the philosophic importance that films of merit may achieve. Since movies are primarily a composite of visual and literary effects, and their auditory accompaniment secondarily, the visual, the literary, and the sonic in them interweave as artful means by which filmmakers express or manifest mythical and philosophical concepts that enrich the cinematic experience they induce. I seek to portray the creativity that constitutes this particular form of life.

In view of the influence that psychoanalytic thinking has had for the last hundred years, we should briefly begin with the theories about mythmaking in the writings of Freud and Jung. Though not wholly representative of the literature in psychology and anthropology, they stand out as thorough attempts worthy of our attention. They often serve as background assumptions that film theorists turn to for insights about the meaningfulness in movies as a whole. Freud's work has been especially suggestive for those who study the relationship between dreaming and the film experience. As a matter of fact, however, Freud only rarely interprets dreams as either the embodiment of myths or the inspiration for filmmaking in general. He thought of dreaming, particularly in its nocturnal mode, as a most obvious access to unconscious processes that occur in daytime consciousness without our always realizing their presence throughout our waking life.

Occasionally, as in his essay on Michelangelo's statue of Moses, Freud deployed his ideas about dreams and the unconscious in an analysis of one or another myth. But even then he usually drew upon Greek and Roman mythologies—in their accounts of Oedipus, Electra, and others—as vehicles that enabled him to create modern myths that he himself fabricated in relation to quasi-scientific opinions of his own about aspects of human psychology. While Freud recognized that the contents of dreams could appear in works of art, notably in films as well as literary narratives, he scarcely probed the possibility that cinematic art may be mythic in itself and inherently similar to dreaming in that respect.

Jung went beyond Freud in speculating about a "collective unconscious" (later referred to as the "objective psyche" of some culture) that revealed itself in dreams and took the form of mythological archetypes recurrent in the history of humanity. Even if one does not agree with either the Jungian or the Freudian dogmas in their totality, as I do not, their emphasis upon dream phenomenology alerts us to its presence in both the film experience and the mythological narratives that different movies diversely present as a basis for such experience.

Watching cinema is like dreaming in several ways. In both circumstances we are mesmerized by our immersion in what is being flashed before us. Sometimes we react negatively to a dream, struggle against some unwelcome segment in its relentless display. We may even force ourselves to awaken from it, like patrons who walk out of the theater. But most often we submit to our passive condition, as spectators who accept and possibly enjoy the relaxation and free entertainment that come to us, without any conscious effort, through dreaming and being asleep. It is as if we are a bemused audience that watches our own dreams as we might watch a film being projected privately for us alone.

There is in the dream condition a degree of what, in my theory of love, I call "bestowal." In dreaming, we are beneficiaries of the gratuitous performance, normally visual but possibly auditory as well, and we allow ourselves to be swept along with a feeling of immediate well-being bestowed upon us that resembles the one that characterizes our nondreaming life at its most creative. Dreams are much more fragmentary and chaotic than our perception of the world when we are awake. But the brain, which never sleeps, makes sense of this situation and compensates for the pervasive obscurities that fill most of our dreaming. We thereby welcome their occurrence, though we may find them disconcerting once we reflect afterward about what we were watching.

Whether or not explicit myths exist in films, they duplicate as a whole these features of the dreaming state. Movies became the principal art form of our age when they did because it was only a hundred or so years ago that technology attained the capacity to combine the making of myths with a vivid simulation in conscious experience of what happens every night when we go to sleep and dream.

At the same time, film also retains the kind of one-to-one contact with a storyteller that some bard or shaman might effect in primitive societies. We gather together with other members of our civilized tribe and fixate upon a single source of excitement and delight. Like the utterance of a bard—even a blind one, as Homer was said to be—the images on-screen seem to be addressing each of us separately despite our collective presence. We identify with the camera inasmuch as we see and hear what it does and wants us to see and hear. The mesmerization in watching movies follows upon this act of identification. We *become* the camera, for the time being and without merging with it in any mystical sense.

While listening to an actual bard or other charismatic speaker, our imagination works as it does in all literary discourse. The words on a page, whether read or intoned by someone else at a distance, or inwardly recited to oneself, have to be processed before we can experience any images that may be relevant to the verbal code from which they derive. Being a visual art, film differs from that—as ordinary life does—insofar as it shows us directly the persons to whom the words refer, and through whom we are to achieve the meaningfulness of thought and sensation we hope to find.

In nonoperatic music an almost infinite realm of meaning can be conveyed, but it is inevitably abstract and its mythic import is limited by a lack of narrative detail that both fictional and nonfictional films can have in varying degrees. Operatic music remedies this, and of course contains no shortage of dramatic intensity. But the sheer expressiveness of the music that propels an opera in the West tends to militate against the kind of realism that is essential, as we shall see, for the making of cinematic myths. Moreover, since opera has always been exclusively a living art (until film changed all that), it had to cope with a difficulty that theatrical media must always face. It arises from the fact that in a play or in an opera the singers always direct their gestures and vocal remarks to each other as characters being portrayed by live people on a stage. They therefore have to use their highly cultivated voices like persons communicating in real life while also subordinating that kind of delivery to the resonance that comes from being a performer whose every utterance must reach out to patrons in the second balcony. The sound in film alters that prerequisite by making nonsinging actors as audible as those who do sing. Nevertheless, since no one sings anywhere except in some performance, the fundamental problem remains intact though certainly manageable.

The necessity of coping with it tends to undermine the credibility and effectiveness of the mythic element in opera, whether on stage or in film. In the hands of inspired composers—Mozart or Verdi, for instance—opera compensates for its limitations by greatly heightened melodrama and vividly outlandish comedy as well as the sublimity of the music. As we all know, many examples of superb mythmaking occur in operas between the seventeenth and twentieth centuries. Film goes further: it transfers the mythological representation out of the theater itself and into the realm of nature and society, where it still takes place aesthetically but can now be observed as if it duplicated what we might encounter in our commonplace immersion in the everyday world of sight and sound.

All the same, we know that basically film is quite unrealistic in its creativity as an art form. Not only are the images enlarged and presented at angles that suit the camera's point of view, as distinct from what we ourselves may have experienced, but also the movement in these "motion" pictures results from a process that is alien to any reality that we are familiar with directly. This bit of truth elicited Henri Bergson's speculations about "the cinematographic effect." In his general distinction between "duration" and "space-time movement," Bergson argues that only the former is true to our actual perception. It occurs in our intuition of time and motion as they flow seamlessly throughout our existence and comprise its very being. In the space-time of clocks or quantitative calculations that belong to science and most conceptualization, Bergson claims, pure temporality or mobility is no longer foremost but rather submerged within a pattern of assumptions and interpretations that evade whatever experience of duration we may possibly have.

According to Bergson, this imposition characterizes the watching of films. He invokes the cinematographic effect in order to illustrate how choppy and strangely contrived is the spatialized movement we readily take as time and mobility although it is very remote from what occurs in intuition attuned to duration, the vital flow of human phenomenology.

I mention this line of thought for a number of reasons. First, Bergson's conception is accurate insofar as we do respond to the cinematography of a film in the manner that he calls the spatialization of time and motion. We see only the *pictures* that are moving, instead of the objects and events they represent. The frames and the images printed on them are organized in a spatial manner that causes us to apprehend some preappointed movement that mechanically appears in each successive showing. Therein resides the creativity of cinematic technique. The question for the philosopher is whether it explains the nature of perception in this medium, or else indicates that what a filmmaker projects upon the screen can only be a distortion of some real-life perception as we intuitively know it to be.

I myself am convinced that Bergson misrepresents the cinematographic effect as well as the aesthetic situation he considers analogous to it. In watching a movie, what we observe is indeed the product of a spatializing of time, inasmuch as there would be no movement for us to see unless there had been the placing of frames on the celluloid, or whatever, all of them designed to succeed each other in space. But it does not follow from this that the motion we see in the projected images is alien to the pure mobility that Bergsonian intuition might afford. In other words, it is through the causality of spatialized time that the cinematographic effect provides us with authentic viewings of motion, and of life, that is no less real and immediate in its fashion than any other experience we may possibly have. Bergson's concept of intuition is therefore mistaken, or at least useless.[1]

Having said this, we can now go on to suggest with greater clarity how it is that the art of film supremely lends itself to the transmittance of mythic themes. By using the technical devices of panning, tracking, zooming, alternating shots that are close, medium, long, and all the rest of normal cinematography, as well as the systematic cutting that goes into the eventual editing, film instills in members of the audience a sense of distance from anything they might see outside the theater or within it before the lights are turned down. This distancing puts the spectators of the finished product into a receptive attitude toward narratives that are unlike life itself precisely *because* they are mythic or include mythic aspects. In being both philosophical as well as overtly contrived and fictional, mythmaking depends upon our imaginative adherence to portrayals and events that we know to be unreal in any other context. At the same time, we are not just lured into but also engrossed by the quasi-realistic character of images that flit before our eyes in semblance of the world outside. The mythic experience combines both characteristics, the unreal as well as the real, the unnatural as well as the natural. In film their visual, sonic, and even kinesthetic components are joined as in no other art form.

Studying film as mythmaking, and mythmaking as part of artistic meaningfulness that film in particular manifests, we should avoid the reductivist approach that critics sometimes employ in their search for one or another fundamental myth. Being very complex constructions, films rarely devote themselves to any single myth or any single pattern of meaning, whether representational or expressional. Most films are ambivalent about the values and the realities they encompass, and virtually all include traces of more than any one myth alone. This is especially evident in the films that interest me in this book. They are offshoots of the variegated history of Western and partly Eastern civilization, and the philosophical scope within them is largely attuned to the diversified myths of love that I have discussed at length in other writings of mine.

Among them are the myths of Tristan and Iseult, Dido and Aeneas, Pygmalion, and Don Juan. These, and multiple variations related to them, have permeated our thought and our arts through an augmentation that comes to us from centuries in our immediate past. Film appears on the scene at a time when the Romantic formulations of those myths reoriented almost everyone's views about the nature and pursuit of love in ways that affected the feelings as well as the behavior of many people. Being the baby of the family, cinema grew up with this evolved approach to affective issues. The philosophical components in it reflect a gamut of mythological probings and the tentative solutions they suggest.

Even a comedy like *The Lady Eve*, whose title seems to limit it to the single myth of Adam and Eve, includes within its narrative progression other myths as well. Moreover, the play, the movie, and the musical versions of George Bernard Shaw's *Pygmalion* mingle elements of the three basic categories of myths to which I referred at the beginning of this chapter: those that deal with creation, the hero's (or heroine's) struggle, and the ideational components in human valuation as a whole. The last of these gives birth to pertinent and pervasive myths about imagination, consummation, the aesthetic, and also idealization itself.

Movies like *The Heiress* or *Washington Square* cannot be fully appreciated without some broadly philosophical recognition of the mythic parameters in each of these modes of mentality. Beyond the ones I have mentioned, there are myths about the meaning of death and of life in our cosmos that dominate the films of Jean Cocteau, Stanley Kubrick, and Federico Fellini as well as hundreds more that my personal selection prevents me from discussing in this book.

Finally, I want to remind the reader of something that Orson Welles said, and that I have cited in other places. Talking about John Ford, whose work he admired and from whose directing he claimed to have learned a great deal, Welles remarked that

Ford was a *maker* of myths whereas he himself was someone who in his films wished to *examine* how mythmaking affects human consciousness. Since he had little of Welles's interest in ideas, Ford might well have spurned the notion that he was a mythmaker at all. He would doubtless have insisted that he was just a craftsman, not even an artist and in fact primarily a storyteller with no philosophical intentions of any sort.

I am willing to accept the Wellesian statement at face value. I infer from it that in the films we will be considering there are different ways of approaching the provocative contents in them. The movies that emanate from Henry James's novels are highly instructive in this regard. In their subtle manner they derive from mythological themes that attained a watershed in the last quarter of the nineteenth century. Through its unique type of artfulness, cinema restores and revives these and other motifs for audiences like ourselves in the twenty-first century.

1

The Lady Eve

Preston Sturges's *The Lady Eve* (1941) is a suitable starting point, if only because it reverberates with the mythology of Adam and Eve in the Book of Genesis. The movie is up-to-date insofar as it discards any of the biblical references to the beginning of life on this planet or the early history of our species, first in the Garden of Eden and then outside. In the categories of myth, this version has no place among those that are cosmological. Instead it limits itself to the mythic dimensions of human good and evil by depicting the progress of a hero who is as simpleminded as pristine Adam and a heroine who resembles Eve in being an exemplar of misbehavior that leads to final knowledge and possible redemption.

The title applies explicitly to the second act of Sturges's tripartite film. During that segment Barbara Stanwyck masquerades as Lady Eve Sidwich. Before and after it, her character's name is Jean Harrington and she talks with a normal American accent instead of the imitation English intonation that fools almost everyone. When she first introduces herself to Charles Pike on the ship, she remarks that her name is really "Eugenia," as if to establish her healthy-minded authenticity. The wealthy hosts and guests at the posh dinner in Connecticut are taken in by Lady

Eve's phony title, a compilation of "Stanwyck" and "sandwich." The single exception is Muggsy (William Demarest, a staple of Sturges's company), who is neither posh nor wealthy.

At a glance and despite her classy speaking voice, which Eve herself later calls talking "like a cockeyed duchess," Muggsy instantly recognizes that she is the woman on the ship. He himself is the snake in the grass, the naysayer who does not believe in love and who rightly discerns how people use it to cheat and deceive those who have fallen under its spell.

Announcing its genre as relevant to the Garden of Eden myth, the movie opens with animation that shows the biblical serpent squirming through the fruit of the tree of the knowledge of good and evil. The randy-looking snake in top hat salivates over apples that alert us to the fact that this will be a story about modern descendants of Adam and Eve. Once the credits have passed, the seductive reptile jiggles a maraca to assure us that we are going to have a jolly time as spectators of the movie.

When the steam-powered launch positions Charles and Muggsy alongside the luxury liner, Jean watches their arrival from an upper deck while she holds a partly eaten apple in her hand. She drops it onto the pith helmet that Charles (Henry Fonda) is wearing as he ascends the ladder and boards the ship. The gesture establishes her as an associate of the serpent, who in the previous animation was also struck by an apple with Eve's name on it. Hitting Charles on the head with forbidden fruit, Jean makes contact with this desirable male. She is already scheming to knock some erotic sense into him.

As often interpreted in the Bible, the serpent is neither male nor female exclusively, but rather a quasi-hermaphroditic combination of both. It is represented not only by Muggsy but also by Emma, the live and evasive snake that Charles brings back from the Amazon. The first time we see Muggsy, he is saying goodbye to a native woman, just before he and Charles get into the boat that will take them to the ship. The woman appears sullen or depressed, and Muggsy terminates his peremptory farewell in a casual, unimpassioned manner that belies any intimacy they may have had. We assume that she has been "his woman" during the year he and Charles have lived on the Amazon, but we can see that he did not love her. As if there were mail delivery in the jungle, he facetiously remarks—as any Don Juan might—that he'll send her a postcard. Not what we would call a demonstration of much affection.

Charles says goodbye to only the head of the expedition and his male colleagues. There is no girlfriend in Charles's life. He receives instruction about the care and feeding of Emma, whom we see squirming in her box. When someone tells him to beware of women, now that he is returning to civilized society, Charles pleasantly insists that he has love for nothing but his scientific research. That means Emma, but he will shortly discover that the animality she represents can elicit in him feelings of a different kind.

In his Adamic innocence, Charles is at first an inexperienced idealist. Pearlie (or is it Purlie?), a crony of Jean and her father whose nickname seems appropriate for a cunning conman who lives by purloining pearls that others value, speaks of Charles as "backwards." When Jean insists that he is a scientist, Pearlie says with reassurance that he knew he was "pec*uu*liar." In their world, Charles surely is. He responds to the allure of slithering creatures like Jean / Eve and Emma, but he always seeks to treat them with protectiveness and respect that he thinks a man should have on all occasions toward the so-called weaker sex. Throughout the film he utters principles of upscale morality that make him seem pompous and a suitable target for ridicule. Like Oliver Alden in the novel George Santayana published in 1935, six years before this movie was made, he is "the last (in the sense of being the ultimate) puritan." But while Santayana's protagonist is not a comic figure, the one that Sturges creates begins as such and then evolves into much more than that.

In a sequence showing the launch as it approaches the ocean liner, Sturges alternates shots of their stacks emitting sounds of greeting and identity. The launch's voice is a high and puerile-seeming whistle; the ship's is a deep and massive blast. The humorous contrast between them duplicates the difference between susceptible but emotionally unawakened Charles and the welter of hovering females onboard who soon make every effort to snare him. Jean is the most astute among them, and she quickly gets this fish to swallow the hook.

Since Muggsy constantly manifests the serpent's lowdown perspective, he serves as a mythic foil to all high-mindedness that is out of touch with the realities of natural life. Through amatory suffering, Charles finally learns how to integrate Muggsy's diabolical message with the more positive possibilities that Jean sincerely, and Eve deceptively, has offered him. As one who knows his way about factual existence, Muggsy plays the same role as Sancho Panza in relation to Don Quijote. The two of them effect a dialectic interchange between realism and idealism that recurs in most buddy films of the last hundred years.

In many of them, the alternate masculine icons compete for an attractive female. The outcome varies. Frequently the idealist, whom we admire for his inherent nobility and staunch pursuit of manly rectitude, wins out. But often he does not. Particularly if he is an artist-type in love with an embodiment of his muse, or else his glamorized memory of their past romance, like Humphrey Bogart in *Casablanca,* he must renounce this love for the exceptional woman and walk off into the desert of his solitary mission. In *The Lady Eve,* the buddies do not compete for Barbara Stanwyck. If anything, Muggsy competes with her for the affective bonding and social education of Charles. In the matrimonial resolution of this film, she wins out over Muggsy as well as Emma, her female rival.

In Genesis the serpent speaks the truth, as he does in later legends as diverse as Goethe's *Faust* and Auden, Kallman/Stravinsky's *The Rake's Progress.* In each case the myth deals with both cognitive and affective enlightenment, and the power that it may create for those who seek it with determination. Adam and Eve having been told that if they eat the fruit of the tree of knowledge of good and evil they will die on that very day, the serpent informs them—as inducement to the goodness he wishes to guide them toward—that this is not true. And it is not. They do not die on that day, but only later when they have been exiled to the wilderness outside Eden. In any event we may plausibly infer that they were never intended to live forever. God implies as much when he says that their disobedience in partaking of the forbidden fruit might now encourage them to eat of the tree of life and so become immortal like himself and all the heavenly host.

Though the serpent misleads the childlike couple by not telling them that their disobedience may result in their being denied the joy and blessedness of living in Eden, he utters nothing that is false about their condition as finite human beings. Not only does Muggsy embody this truth-telling function at all times, but he also has the last word in the film. He emerges from Jean's stateroom, stares at the camera and at us, and reiterates his firm belief (which we know to be correct) that she and Eve are "*positively* the same dame."

What exactly does that mean? Is Muggsy saying merely that Jean has been masquerading as Eve, acting as if she were an English aristocrat, pretending to be someone she is not? Or, less obviously but more suggestively, is he remarking upon her identity as an individual in whom two different personae reside, one earnestly struggling for liberation from her previous crookedness and the other capable of carrying out the conniving plot we've just observed? There is no contradiction in saying yes to both questions. When Jean becomes starry-eyed in love, she has the same optimistic innocence as Charles. But even then she knows how dangerous her attachment can be to him, as well as to herself. In acting as she does after he has harmed her, she reveals what was in her as the same dame all along.

The serpent in Genesis is more than just an informant about human nature and mortality. It is itself the creator of what, in the myth, is considered an ever-present hazard that Adam and Eve must forever confront once they attain knowledge about it. The serpent embodies the possible harm that emanates from the alluring things in nature that can seduce creatures like this man and woman into breaking the prime commandment God has ordained for their governance. Though the serpent has itself probably eaten from the forbidden tree, it may see no harm in conveying to these newborn human beings the perilous wisdom it has garnered from its own experience. Similarly, Jean's transformation into vengeful Lady Sidwich is motivated by her self-righteous belief that Charles deserves to be punished. He has wronged her by not accepting the genuine love that she felt for him, and never before in her life. With the venomous logic of the snake, she feels this justifies her retaliation.

Film critics and others who loosely rely upon Freudian or Jungian theory have readily assumed that the image of the snake must symbolize not only libidinal sexuality but also fears about it that many people have. From that it takes only a little step to interpret Jean's revulsion toward Emma as an indication of problems she suffers in her sex life. She is thought to be troubled either by her rampant promiscuity or else by her virginal horror of carnal intercourse. But though Jean is overtly flirtatious with Charles without actually going to bed with him, as she teasingly suggests early on in order to augment and not yet satisfy his hopes, we have no reason to conclude that she has a deeply rooted dread of sex, or any sense of having failed at it. Such ideas do not belong to her character, or to Charles's. They are neither dualistic Christians nor proto-Kantian prudes. A Freudian or Jungian reading will not take us very far, I believe.

In Genesis we are told that animosity between the snake and the female descendants of Eve is part of the punishment God metes out to our primal parents. For the mythic purposes of the film, that alone fully explains why Jean is terrified at the mere sight of Emma and rightly suspicious of Muggsy throughout.

When her newfound love has seized her, Jean tells her father that Charles has touched something in her heart: "I think I'm in love with the poor fish, snakes and all." In Emma we may see the rare, precious, and totally emancipated female that Jean has been and wants to remain, but without the immoral implication of having been a con artist. She recoils from acting with Charles like just another Emma, regardless of how much she resembles her. Sex is not the problem, only its proper administration.

Note that when Jean leads Charles to his own stateroom and he invites her in to meet Emma, she cheerfully takes this as a sexual overture. "That's a new one, isn't it?" she says, as if he had offered to show her his "etchings"—or rather his penis, to which he has given this nickname, Emma, oddly female though it is. Seeing the little snake, however, Jean shrieks and runs off in a panic.

Previously, when her father remarked about her wearing the same outfit despite the long time she and Charles were in her cabin to find a new pair of shoes, Jean replies: "I'm lucky to have this one on. Mr. Pike has been up the river for a year." If Charles had in fact ripped off her clothes, she would have been in the condition of the biblical Eve. She obviously wants to foster that image in the young man. The unnerving presence of Emma interferes with her plan. While Emma represents not only a biologic vitality in Jean but also the sliminess of her former existence, she fancies that her love for a decent, innocent, and also wealthy person like Charles will enable her to change. "I'd give a lot to be—well, I mean I'm *going* to be," she tells her father after love has lit its flame, "exactly the way he thinks I am, the way he'd like me to be."

Once Charles has revealed that he cannot comprehend the truthfulness in her stated desire to cleanse her previous dishonesty through sexual love for him, she turns on this potential mate with all the fury of a woman scorned by his refusal to help her reform. She reacts as Potiphar's wife in the Bible would have, or as do any number of evil witches in world mythology. In Hitchcock's *Notorious*, produced a few years later, the Ingrid Bergman character responds to a similar situation in a somewhat varied manner. Until her lover, Cary Grant, alters his attitude toward her past waywardness, she morosely succumbs to its permanence in her life. Emma is the devil Jean wants to put behind her but cannot at this stage of her moral development. During preparations for the party in honor of Eve, Emma coils around the butler's lower leg as if in a preview of how Eve will guilefully twist the menfolk and their wives about her little finger. Emma's tenaciousness is, as we learn, an ambiguous resource in Eve as well as Jean.

The thematic progression largely consists of the ups and downs of Charles and Jean/Eve. The slapstick vaudeville of Charles falling down time and again is so outrageously presented that we can't help laughing on each occasion. Except for his final fall, when Jean trips him a second time on the same ship and in the same way, his falling down always has a different physical configuration. That is why we never weary of these repeated and all-too-obvious allusions to the fall of Adam. The clownish pratfalls, one after another within a few minutes during the formal dinner, reach the peak of their comic crescendo when Charles in his pajamas steps off the post-wedding train, after having pulled the emergency cord, one assumes, and falls flat on his back in a puddle of mud.

Interlarded with these bits of wonderfully low humor are the numerous times we see Charles going downstairs in the ship and at home, as if in anticipation of the final and rewarding descent that he will experience at the end of the movie. On the ship, after he has fallen to the floor the second time, the trope completes itself. He and Jean fall into each other's arms, kiss, and make up in a passionate embrace that glues them together securely. They then run downstairs hand in hand and effect their total reconciliation in the privacy of her cabin.

As I will be arguing, Charles's repeated falling is consonant with, and parallel to, the pattern of Jean/Eve's descent. Though his falls are psychological as well as physical, and though he learns about life and about women as a result of them, he is not yet—and probably never will be—the profound human being that she is. From beginning to end, he must be seen as a somewhat passive object of desire that the female pursues in her role as questing huntress who must deploy focused intellect and inventive maneuvering to catch her prey. On the other hand, Charles is not just a stuffed shirt or archetypal product of upperclass stupidity.

In his essay written for the DVD version of *The Lady Eve*, James Harvey suggests that Charles remains "unbelievable" throughout his transformations: "It is neither as a character nor as an embodied idea that we experience him in the movie."[1] That seems too extreme to me. In his book *Romantic Comedy in Hollywood, Lubitsch to Sturges*, Harvey comes closer to the truth when he detects in Charles a succession of three almost different kinds of men. The first is "the absentminded professor, the male virgin with arcane intellectual interests possessed of a nearly unshakable equanimity as he is cheated, mocked, tripped, dragged down three flights of stairs"; the second is "smug and self-righteous"; the third "who appears triumphantly at the very end, seems for his brief moment on the screen to be just what a romantic lead should be."[2]

While realizing that these three are not inconsistent with each other and that Sturges makes us feel their rightness in a single character, Harvey fails to appreciate the continuity among these transformations. From the start, perspicacious Jean sees their possible unity as a characterological capacity in Charles. He certainly has his comic doltish side, but he is nevertheless a young and serious-minded scientist, like Cary Grant—who also keeps falling down—in *Bringing Up Baby*. By the end of the story Charles has learned how to live, and he succeeds in winning the heroine's heart in a romantic context that no longer depends upon his affluence. After the curtain comes down and Jean has finished working on him, Charles will doubtless turn into a wiser and more estimable person.

Embodying a more vital force of nature, Jean retains an innate nobility throughout. She demonstrates eventually the significance of her self-imposed title of "Lady" Eve. From the very start, she has the aristocratic bearing of a lady and all the assuredness of the mythical female who is the source of all humanity outside Eden. When she falls in love and then fails, at the end of the first act, she does not sulk as Charles does in his reaction to both falling and failing. Instead Jean behaves forcefully. In response to the pain she feels, she changes from seducer Jean to regal Eve; she schemes to find a new way to impose herself upon Charles; and she does so through hatred that expresses an inverted form of the love still operative in her.

"I need him like the axe needs the turkey," she says at this point. In rejecting Jean as well as Eve, Charles runs away from the need that he has for the woman who is both Jean and Eve, and with whom he has fallen in love. Being a deeper and more imaginative person than him, Jean / Eve accepts the hazards she must face and stays the course without knowing what its culmination may be.

Correspondingly, her stages of decline are not physical. We never see her fall to the ground. At the outset, standing on the deck with her father, she towers over Charles below. She is sophisticated in the ways of the world, and he is not; she has a plan of action, and he climbs onboard with no awareness of his coming subjugation. Yet Jean is already a fallen woman, an artful gambler on the prowl for a sucker whose money she can acquire by cheating him. Being *la traviata*, as in Verdi, she understands the mythic value of love better than anyone else and pays the price for it as incurred by her previous way of living.

From her initial state as a clever and worldly woman, Jean descends to Charles's level just by falling in love with him. Their newfound ecstasy declares itself well before their romantic evening together in the moonlight on the prow of the ship. The day after they meet, both are mentally adrift within the exhilarating world they have now fabricated for each other. At breakfast by themselves, Charles absentmindedly orders a scotch and soda. Jean kids him, and with good humor Charles immediately recognizes the inappropriateness of what he has said. When the waiter suggests a remedy for a hangover, Charles remarks: "He doesn't understand." Jean does. She feels the same sense of all-engulfing oneness as Charles.

After Jean lured him into her cabin the night before, to get a new pair of shoes, and then later on to snuggle after Emma has frightened her, she sauntered arm in arm on the deck with her catch in a way that proclaims to everyone that she is succeeding where all the other young women could not. But in the breakfast scene I just mentioned, there is no public display or need to flaunt erotic superiority. It is from that zenith of mutual attachment that Jean plummets once Charles gets the photographic evidence about her shady existence.

I will return to that scene presently, but here we should note that this fall precedes another one of even greater significance. Having been rejected by Charles, Jean falls out of love and plunges into her search for revenge. Though the latter is correlative to her unsatisfied longing for affection, it also contravenes it. On the honeymoon train after she has legally acquired Charles, she allows her moral debasement to continue as far as it will go. Once her hateful plan has been fulfilled, however, and Charles has ended up in the mud, we see her mentality change as she watches him through the compartment window and then slowly, regretfully, pulls down the curtain. The axe having fallen on the turkey's neck, there is nothing more to be attained in that direction. She has vented her anger and lingering indignation. Thereafter she moves upward, refusing to take any alimony, contriving to reappear as Jean on the same ship as Charles, and then causing them both to relive the past in a new and happier fashion.

The mythological motif of protagonists falling and struggling to rise again reappears as well in other films of Preston Sturges. In *Sullivan's Travels* Joel McCrea intentionally falls from his eminence as a highly successful film director, meets a down and out actress (Veronica Lake), takes her along with him to live like the downtrodden poor, and is later pushed into his outdoor pool by her. He pulls her in, and his butler and valet do the same to each other. In *The Palm Beach Story,* McCrea falls down a whole flight of stairs in his haste to stop his wife after she claims to have fallen out of love for him.

In *The Lady Eve,* Charles's habitual falling and final depressiveness when he feels he has been deceived a second time are given a counterpoint in the shots of his jolly but graceless father (Eugene Pallette) marching down the long stairway in his house while intoning a lower-class drinking song. Though his affection for Eve later enables the father to show himself at his best, before that happens we see him fall into to a state of childhood, clamoring like a helpless boy when his breakfast has been delayed. From that nadir of infantile behavior, he rises at the end of the film to a magnanimous height from which he graciously encourages Eve to soak Charles (and, implicitly, their entire family) for all the money she can get.

Sturges relentlessly organizes the pattern of these ups and downs with a rapid but steady rhythm that is comedic in and of itself. Even Muggsy the snake accidentally falls into the vegetation outside the country house. We laugh in recognition of the filmmaker's technical mastery of the genre he has chosen. It likewise shows itself in the sharp and witty repartee among his characters, and in his many private jokes. For instance, Charles's family name is Pike, and though he is very rich, he is referred to as a "poor fish" who has just emerged from the Amazon River. Muggsy facetiously tells the bursar on the ship that cardsharks are swimming alongside—presumably because they hope to devour the pike that is in the water with them. Muggsy's very name is a joke, since he is not a "mug" as crooks use that term (meaning a likely victim), but rather a mug in the sense of being a man who is rough and abrasive. And throughout all this virtuosity, Sturges's expertise as both director and scriptwriter actively produces the mythological import that resides within the fundamental structure of his movie.

This import appears most fully in the scene that occurs on the morning after Jean and Charles declare in the moonlight their love for each other. Floating in a balloon of euphoria that will be punctured presently, Charles has been handed a photograph of Jean, her father, and their accomplice Gerald that immediately puts him into an abysm of utter desolation. On the back of the photo an authoritative-sounding paragraph details the criminality of the gang. Shattered by what he reads and believes, and has good reason to believe, Charles hastens to the bar, where he orders a scotch and soda to steady his nerves. This harks back to the previous morning, when an identical order for breakfast signified his amatory but mindless detachment from ordinary life. Now he has to brace himself for its cruel reality.

Surprised to find him at the bar and looking as forlorn as he does, Jean asks whether something is troubling him. He responds by inquiring whether he has cause to be troubled. She answers yes, and then delivers her honest and forthright lines about the dangers he faces in loving a woman like herself. As part of his education, she imparts a truth about women that he has never learned and that she can teach him better than any other person he is likely to meet: "The best ones ["girls," as she calls them] aren't as good as you probably think they are, and the bad ones aren't as bad, not nearly as bad." It is the same message that Oscar Wilde propounds as the upshot of his play *Lady Windemere's Fan*.

The scene is pivotal because the message in Jean's statement permeates the movie as a basic truth about human nature. With his slow and earnest disposition, enacted to perfection by Fonda, Charles's research on the Amazon has not prepared him for this kind of knowledge. He needs the course of instruction that Jean, as well as Eve, will provide throughout the rest of the story. The scene itself demonstrates Sturges's inspired filmmaking. With clarity of intention and absolute control that remind us of Mozart's agility in all his operatic music, Sturges moves from slapstick to romantic ebullience and then to utterly convincing emotional pain without ever missing a beat. Stanwyck, at the pinnacle of her dramatic talent, registers the excruciating heartache that any girl or woman would have in being crushed at the very moment that rebirth through love had seemed within her grasp. When she appears on deck two scenes later as the ship is landing in New York, stiff within her haughty fur coat, we see how she has turned into a frozen pillar of hatred and how greatly she has been hurt.

Muggsy might well have agreed with Jean's dictum about herself and her fellow females. Moreover, he thinks "they" are all the same. But since he has never experienced love for any of them, he cannot appreciate the profundity of Jean's remark. If the good ones are not as good, or the bad ones as bad, as anything a well-intentioned but uninformed man like Charles believes, the moral differences within female sexual conduct are much less pronounced than received opinion always contends. This humane and pluralistic outlook has never penetrated as hard a skull as Muggsy has.

In the version that Genesis recounts, Eden is a paradise on earth. The animals live in peace with each other, and, far from being predators who stand aloof, the human beings commune as equals with all the rest of creation. They belong to the family of life as St. Francis imagined it when he communed with the birds and spoke of Brother Sun and Sister Moon, as in Franco Zeffirelli's mythological film with that title. Adam gives names to the other animals, and Eve does not shy away from conversing with the well-spoken reptile. In Orson Welles's conception, this image of a golden age, a period of harmonious gentleness that constitutes "the good old days," manifests what he calls a "myth of the past." As I have tried to depict in an earlier book, that Wellesean image of innocence becomes an ideational ingredient in some of his most accomplished films.[3] It is not the perspective in Sturges's work. He is more modern, and even more modernist, than Welles.

The all-inclusive condition that Sturges presents is entangled with duplicity and gnarled with undesirable elements of humankind that defeat any idea of a good old time when everything was fine. Though Charles has a sterling character beneath his bourgeois-minded veneer, he lies to Jean after he has read the incriminating paragraph on the back of the photo. To save face, he claims that he knew all along that she and her father were crooks. And beneath Jean's disappointment, so affecting as Stanwyck conveys it in her crushed though only slightly modulated facial gestures when Charles has rejected her on that occasion, there remains a lingering faith in the mythology of reciprocal love that belies her past experience of the world. Could she really have thought that dalliance with Charles after they have known each other for only a day or two would persuade him that she is now wholly altered from what she has been? Even the biblical Eve would not have been that naive. In his merciless though humorous demeanor, Sturges brings the myth into the present by imposing upon it the confusing complexity of our advanced reality as the human beings we are now. To that extent, he is possibly more of a realist than Welles was.

One of the ways Sturges applies his sense of complexity is through his use of mirrors. Stanley Cavell, in two essays, and Marian Keane, in her often excellent DVD commentary on *The Lady Eve,* claim that these mirrors reflexively signify the cinematic medium itself as it copies reality within the frame of the camera's lens. Keane specifically states that, in the sequence that ends with Jean tripping up Charles the first time, her use of a hand mirror to see people and events in the dining room mimics what a filmmaker does in observing and directing everything that happens in a film.[4] Suggestive as this kind of interpretation may be, it neglects the fact that photographic images are quite different from images in a mirror.

Both types are transformations—neither is a literal duplication of anything in the world—but they nevertheless rely upon dissimilar types of transformational imagery. Existing within a medium that is either a fiction or a recording (as in a documentary), the photographic image can only provide *representations* of actual events. It is not a re-presenting of what previously occurred in experience. Only within a play of imagination can one person (the filmmaker, in particular) communicate through his or her medium to other persons that constitute an audience attuned to the artistic product they are experiencing. Mirror images are not the same.

Those who make a mirror, or arrange for a machine to make it, are not part of any communication between themselves and the person who looks into that mirror. Distorted as it may be, a mirror image is a technological, even automatic, reflection of the actuality one sees in looking at a mirror. Mirrors can show us only a special segment of our visual world. There is indeed a likeness, often a striking and possibly unique likeness, between the mirror image and that of which it is an image. And one might say something comparable about photographic images. Still they, as opposed to mirror images, belong to the inherent nature of a creative art form—photography or cinema. In itself a mirror is not an art form at all.

All the same, we must recognize, and account for, the fact that mirrors are often seen in movies, even more so than in paintings. They rarely occur in stage plays. In the theater there is always the danger that a mirror might reflect back to people in the audience what they themselves look like. That would be a distraction and could diminish the play's attempt to "hold up a mirror to nature," as literature does, without presenting it in a literal or iconographic sense. Though many films resemble plays, the former arise from a mode of imagination that is not activated by the latter. Mirrors are frequently prominent in films because they provide a picturization that is *akin* to what appears in photography as a whole. That allows them to blend unobtrusively into the visual structure of a movie.

When this happens, mirrors increase the spatial properties of almost any cinematic setting. The silver screen is a cropping of reality just as the frame of a painting or the border of a stage is. But while the spectators of a play are looking into the depth of the stage merely by watching what is being performed on it, both painting and film are two-dimensional even when they represent the third dimension. Being instruments of refraction, mirrors *enlarge* our field of perception, backward in depth as well as forward and sometimes to a simulacrum of infinity. They thereby afford purely spatial opportunities that film can beneficially employ despite its primal divergence from mirrors themselves.[5]

With this in mind, we do best to disregard much of what is said about self-reflexivity and orient our analysis in other ways entirely. Instead of treating the inclusion of mirrors in a film as revealing the nature of filmmaking itself, we should try to see how mirrors function in the psychodynamics of some narrative.

Some directors—William Wyler and Jean Renoir, among many others—are especially adept at using mirrors to advantage in their mise-en-scène. In each case, we need to determine how the extra space afforded by a mirror image augments the meaningfulness of a shot.

For instance, what exactly is happening in that scene when Jean looks into her compact's hand mirror and describes, sometimes even addresses in imagination, the persons she is studying by means of it? For one thing, she is sizing up the inadequacies of her competitors there in the dining hall who might also hope to marry a moneyed and good-looking man like Charles. She does this by peering into a mirror that reflects not herself but only the rivals, as if she has lost her own reflection. That loss happens to people in various legends when their souls have been stolen by the Evil One, the devil. In this context, the loss of her image enables Jean to be quasi-invisible. She can see the other women while they cannot see her seeing them.

There is something diabolical about that, but we know that Jean has not yet lost her soul: she is far too bright and buoyant. On the contrary, as the film scholar Martin Marks has suggested to me, Jean holding her mirror shows her to be a person who has the world in the palm of her hand. The mirror is for her like the field glass of a general who is surveying enemy troops. Without disclosing what she is doing, since people think she is looking at her face, she has the advantage of observing what is going on all around and even behind her. It is as if she has eyes in the back of her head, like Argus in Greek mythology. And just as the paragraph on the back of her group photo proffers crucial intelligence, so too does the mirror yield battlefield data that eventuate in Jean's tripping Charles when he walks past her table.

Later in the film, Sturges uses mirrors for even more elaborate effects. After Jean has told her father Harry that she is in love with Charles, he stands behind her in one scene as she puts on her shoes while looking into floor-length mirrors. The images are replicated as father and daughter speak to one another through the mirrors that successively mirror themselves. The two talk about the consequences of her romance and discuss Charles's possible reaction to her telling him the truth about her involvement in the gang. After the issue has been raised, Jean finishes getting dressed and looks her father in the eye as she agrees to tell Charles nothing until they leave the ship.

This exchange of imagery as well as language illustrates the reverberating importance of Jean's relationship to her father. It shows how much he still means to her, and how greatly she accepts responsibility for having curtailed his occupational behavior. Still, when they were before the mirrors, they were talking to their images *in* the mirrors. They were not talking directly to each other, as they later do, and as most others do when they converse. What is the significance of that?

As I have suggested elsewhere, Alfred Hitchcock often conveys the nature of a conversation through over-the-shoulder shots that indicate in turn the point of view of each speaker as well as the participation of both in this communal, joint event. Sturges's method is quite different, and even in the latter part of the scene his camera shows only the profiles of the two conversants. Moreover, by having father and daughter at first address the infinitely receding mirror images of them both, it prepares us for the extent to which their ability to communicate will now and forever be altered by Jean's affair. Not only will it be impossible for them to remain accomplices, or talk person to person and face to face as they used to, but also their intimate relationship as parent and offspring will henceforth be sullied by their elusive images of each other.

The consequences for Harry are as profound as they are for Jean. Though he is a supremely adept technician in his livelihood as clever and dishonest cardplayer, he has nothing like the range of feeling and imagination that Jean has. He is not a magician, as some commentators have suggested. He is instead an embodiment of the mythic trickster in world literature, a person whose acts of common immorality we are expected to condemn while also enjoying his bravado and uncanny astuteness.

Harry knows his shortcomings and accepts them openly. When Jean suddenly awakes frightened by a nightmare about Emma, Harry sits on her bed and manages to comfort her with a card trick that she finds incredible. With forthright realization of his limitations, Harry points out that "you don't really need it. It's just virtuosity."

Jean then asks Harry to tell her fortune. While he is neither a magician nor an inhabitant of a magical world somehow comparable to the world of movies, as Cavell and Keane fancifully believe, he is certainly proficient as a card cheat. It therefore seems appropriate for Jean to identify him with an equally successful class of professional crooks, those who pretend to see someone's future by reading it in the person's playing cards. Harry does not, however, respond to Jean's request to read her future. As a devoted father, he has no inclination to deceive her. The rest of the movie goes on to demonstrate his total inability to understand this remarkable child he has brought into the world.

As far as we can tell, Harry is Jean's sole begetter. No mother is ever mentioned. Like Brünnhilde in Wagnerian mythology, and Athena in the Greek, Jean is the wunderkind who has sprung from the forehead of her resourceful father. Like those two divinities, she is also capable of defying and even thwarting him. Soon after this scene, Jean outswindles Harry at the card table in an attempt to restore his ill-gotten winnings to victimized Charles. She then taunts him: "Know any other games, Harry?" She would seem to know them all. She has access to greater awareness in life than anything he can teach her. And neither will she hesitate to use against him, if necessary, whatever he has instilled in her. As she says: "I'm not your daughter for free, you know!"

In particular, Jean's father has little comprehension of the sexual love that Jean experiences with Charles. Harry lacks her strong and resilient sense of what comes naturally. In the world of Verdi's melodramas, Jean would be not only a fallen Violetta, except that her love does culminate in marriage, but also a Gilda in her relation to her corrupt and ineffectual father Rigoletto. When Jean tells Harry that Charles is in love with her, he assumes that she has merely set up the rich guy and will now help the syndicate take his money from him. Neither Harry nor Gerald can believe, at first, that Jean has herself fallen in love with the elected mug.

The bonding and the social implications of that attachment exceed the game playing with which the two male sharpies are familiar. Harry sees no place for himself as a father-in-law or even grandfather in a household that inevitably denies him the excitement of robbing some unsuspecting sucker. In the finale, however, when Jean trips Charles for the second time, Harry is in on the maneuver. He sits at the table and then stands next to Jean as if everything has remained the same since the first time. Indeed nothing that is fundamental or permanent has changed in the love between Jean and Charles, the wounds of their mutual self-education having more or less healed. But Harry is outside all of that. Though Charles hurriedly promises him that they will play "lots and lots of cards," Harry will have to spend the rest of his life by himself in the family business, cruising on one ship after another, endlessly alone in his mythic role like the Wandering Jew or the Flying Dutchman and his crew of loveless ghosts.

The hostility Muggsy feels toward Jean/Eve throughout the movie is also directed toward her father as the chief con man on the ship. In another mirror scene, Muggsy warns Charles about the gang while Charles is shaving. Charles defends Harry through the mirror before turning his face and talking with Muggsy head-on. Neither then nor at any later stage do the two of them reach agreement about the people with whom Charles is now associating. In several aspects, Muggsy and Harry are very much alike. When Muggsy plays cards with Gerald, his intuitions warn him that Gerald cheates. Muggsy claims that he can spot a "cold" deck just by getting his mitts on one. After Charles and Jean live together, in some nonexistent sequel we can imagine, Charles will doubtless fire Muggsy on the grounds that he no longer needs his nannylike protection and Muggsy will team up with Harry and Gerald. Unlike Charles's father or any of the other characters, these three are attuned to the dark forces in the world as it is. Muggsy sneaks out of Jean's cabin in the closing moments as if he knows already that he will be excluded from the second Eden, idyllic but unreal, that they are beginning to create there.

This secondness in their relation to each other pertains to what Cavell calls movies of remarriage that constitute a genre of Hollywood film production in the 1930s and 1940s. Like various others, I have some doubts about the defining properties of this alleged genre, within the rubric of which Cavell analyzes *The Lady Eve*.[6] The film does contain a marriage whose wedding ceremony we see on-screen, but the marriage is not consummated until the very end and after the intervening discussions about annulment are dropped when Jean decides to make her final effort to succeed as a conventionally married woman. There is no divorce or literal second marriage, only a completion of the first one that brings about the culminating oneness. These details do not match Cavell's criteria for a comedy of remarriage. He nonetheless considers them close enough to be suggestive of what he deems generic in the film's thematic totality.

I myself find other features in the film that seem to me more relevant than the notion of remarriage. Since that never occurs in *The Lady Eve*, the entire emphasis falls upon the vagaries of romance before, and reromance after, marriage. In its first and second segments, Charles falls in love with Jean and then with Eve. Though puzzled at first by their physical resemblance, he has no difficulty with this alteration in his choice of whom to love once he has been told that the women are twin sisters. Consequently, one can say that for him there are two different romances that he experiences. Yet we know that Jean and Eve are one and the same woman, and we have seen how she has consciously evoked both of these romances through her great cleverness and erotic know-how. The first romance leads to her also falling in love; and deceptive though she is in the second one, the viewers' likely acquiescence to romantic ideology can cause them to believe that love, or at least love-hate, is functioning there as well. If, on the other hand, we are pessimists like Marcel Proust, we might prefer to repeat his cynical statement about men, throughout their successive love affairs, always falling in love with the same woman. That highlights the identity between romance and reromance.

Since Jean/Eve is positively the same dame who really loves Charles, Proust's dictum does not strictly apply to her. Of course, Proust might deny that she is truly in love. In superficial ways, she does resemble the scheming females in his fiction—Odette, for example—who only pretend romantic attachment for the sake of deluding one or another susceptible male. But in being a fallen woman who finds redemption through authentic love, Jean/Eve transcends the Proustian model. She has at her command intellectual and emotional qualities that none of the women in Proust can muster.

Just as Charles learns about women, the bad ones as well as the good, through his involvement with her, so too does Jean undergo a sentimental education of her own. The prior levels of predatory manipulation followed by sexual love followed by the agony of frustration followed by enmity and revenge result for her in interpersonal love that may very well lead to marital happiness since the man that she has chosen undergoes a parallel development.

In Sturges's vision, one romance alone would not have sufficed for so profound a retelling of the Garden of Eden myth. In *The Palm Beach Story*, he amplifies the principle of doubleness in *The Lady Eve* by having as its denouement two sets of identical twins. After the original married couple separate because the wife is dissatisfied with her husband's financially troubled life, they eventually reunite in what can be thought of as a remarriage after additional (and duplicate) lovers marry the siblings of each of them. We even see the main protagonists in a second wedding ceremony, standing next to their twins, who are having their first. Yet smart and winsome as the initial wife is in that movie, she never attains the stature of Jean/Eve. Perhaps because the idea of the identical twins is so clearly a gimmick, a kind of biological deus ex machina, there is little scope for the imaginative brilliance that Jean/Eve has, or for the personal growth she thereby achieves.

In *The Great McGinty* and *Hail the Conquering Hero,* Sturges plays artfully with the mythic theme of people who pretend to be persons they are not. In *Sullivan's Travels* this motif is present in the desire of its protagonist to learn by imitation about the life of others who are not like himself. He has been favored with pampered upbringing and an elite education—somewhat on the order of Charles in *The Lady Eve,* and Sturges himself as a young man. In his devotion to aesthetic truth, the fictional director wants to make a realistic movie about the poor and underprivileged. His masquerading as a hobo is an inverted image of Jean/Eve's deceptive journey among the well-heeled mugs in Connecticut. The great difference lies in the fact that she, like her prototype in the Bible, is a fertility goddess whose romantic awakening eventuates in the marital institution that has been chosen for the reproduction of the species.

The moviemaker in *Sullivan's Travels* is a man in a mythmaking profession that has been dominated by men and congruent with artistic aspirations that compensate members of the male sex for lacking the creative potential that most women possess just in being wives and mothers. Jean/Eve outshines everyone else because she is so completely an expression of this natural capability while having as well the artifice and skill that is required by all professionals as a whole, male and female.

When Welles addressed the myth of the past as he saw it, he studied it by reference to a departed "merrie England" still present in the world of Shakespeare's Falstaff, or in an early and magnificent period of American life during which the Ambersons savor their social prominence. In doing so, Welles applied the story of Adam and Eve in the Garden of Eden to these former moments of history that then suffered a fall in their essential values. Sturges makes no such attempt. Though he was to the manor born and, as a Rooseveltian traitor to his class, could ridicule the foibles of those who inhabit grand estates, he puts very little satire or social commentary into *The Lady Eve*. His domain is the human heart, not an era in American or English history, or in general the problems of Western civilization. In *Sullivan's Travels* Sturges does go in search of socioeconomic truths about the impoverished in the United States, but the outcome is not in fact sociological or political, and therefore it remains less compelling and less immediate than the witty thrusts in the comedic screwiness of *The Lady Eve*.

All the same, Welles and Sturges were alike in many respects. They both had highly cultivated parents who imbued them with a love of the fine arts at an early age; they developed the taste and outlook of aesthetic virtuosi; at a time when it was very hard to do so, they became film directors as an extension of their literary talents—Welles as an actor who also writes, Sturges as the writer of his own screenplays. Moreover, they each had meteoric success in their beginnings at Hollywood, and then a rapid decline from which they never fully recovered. As I mentioned in my book on Ingmar Bergman, they both resembled him in these regards, except for the last one. Bergman alone managed to survive the hazards of being an independent-minded filmmaker during the period when the studios were all-powerful.[7]

It may only be a coincidence, but still we should note that 1941 is the year in which *The Lady Eve* and also *Citizen Kane* were made. In their alternative disposition, they reflect much of what was happening in Hollywood as the 1930s progressed. *Citizen Kane* can be seen as presupposing the populist, New Dealish, and romantically democratic films of Frank Capra and others. The protagonist in the latter was usually an innocent outsider who somehow rises to political eminence but then must contend with the less-than-ideal forces that run things in a modern state. In his negative response to that reality, Welles chooses a flamboyant tycoon who has inherited enormous wealth and considers himself a superior person worthy of taking control of "the people" and their public institutions because they are inherently beneath him.

Where the Capra-type movie idealizes some ordinary plebeian who epitomizes the unquenchable wisdom of the masses, Welles makes a film in which his imitation of William Randolph Hearst proclaims that through his newspapers he can see to it that people will think "what I tell them to." For his part, Sturges avoids such issues entirely. He works best within the finely developed vehicle of the madcap farce whose leading lady—Katharine Hepburn or Irene Dunne, for example—outwits the typical American male in her attempt to steer him into the mutual bliss of marital bondage. *The Lady Eve*, however, like

Shakespeare's comedies of masquerade, demonstrates how much anguish and inward distortion a heroic female must endure, and how ruthlessly she may visit her conniving intellect upon some hapless, though ultimately fortunate, male.

Sturges's success in this field issues from his daring juxtaposition of clashing affective colors that most Hollywood directors kept discretely separate on their palette. Though enacted with great insight by Stanwyck, Jean's display of jubilant emotion when she feels herself in love with Charles is standard fare for romantic comedies of the period. But the feelings that exist when Jean is rejected and cheapened, as she says, belong to human drama of another kind. Her pitiless revenge is exquisitely combined with a concatenation of absurdities that enable us to accept the underlying sadism with untrammeled glee. When we have had our fill, Sturges shifts again and impresses us with the cathartic image of Jean's self-abnegation as she refuses any alimony and throws herself (or rather, her unerring foot) at Charles's feet.

This versatile ability to change directions in the narrative, and in our reaction to it, corresponds to the startling utterances, back and forth, that Sturges puts into the mouths of even his minor characters. In tiny, vignette-like scenes, some of the best moments are given to the staid butler as he is besmirched by misdirected frosting, to the cook who is maddened by the ridiculous Sidwich coat of arms that he is expected to emblazon on the festive cake, or to Muggsy when he acts violently insulted because the waiter on the ship reads a prearranged menu to him or because the butler addresses him by his first name (Ambrose, which Muggsy probably considers highfalutin, though the butler does not).

This freedom of Sturges's imagination keeps us alert and delighted while it also overcomes problems in the staging of various scenes. On the ship, for example, there are important occasions when Charles has a rendezvous with Jean for which he shows up before she does. That allows her to sashay on screen with the comfortable assurance that the man in her life has been waiting for her. The first time, her meeting with him is joyous for both of them; the second time, it turns into agony for each. In itself, the contrast between the two scenes creates a dramatic effect.

But what is the director to do with Fonda as he waits for Stanwyck? Sturges handles the matter by having him ogle some girls who walk by on the deck. Yet that is not enough, and so Sturges introduces an oddly attired man in shorts and a striped T-shirt who is carrying what might be a fishing net on a long pole. He passes calmly in front of Charles, initially in one direction, and a few seconds later in the opposite direction. In the second scene, he walks by again, together with another man, both carrying strange objects—a harpoon, perhaps, and a stack of plates. All this is wholly irrelevant to the plot.

In presenting these bizarre situations as he does, Sturges fills up the interval until Jean appears by simply jabbing the audience with a sense of the absurdity in life. We laugh at these extraneous walk-ons precisely because they are extraneous, and therefore laughable. Horace, the first name of Charles's father, is itself ludicrous in view of the bearer's unpoetic character. In the scene outside the mansion in Connecticut when he has his childish fit because no breakfast appears before him, two supernumeraries we've not yet seen pass in front of the camera at different moments. One of them is carrying a sizable potted plant in each arm; the other is a piano tuner in search of a piano. Neither can help Horace get his breakfast. With the humor of logical inconsistency, the first man remarks "I cannot speak"; but Horace's irrational and frenetic hope that either of them might manage to provide him with something to eat is itself funny. It is the funniness of a "nuthouse," which is the term that Horace used earlier to describe his crazy home with two identical telephones side by side on a mantelpiece though only one of them is in operation. It is a place where anyone might show up and even pretend, as Eve does, that he or she is an influential member of English nobility.

Sturges conveys the aesthetic richness in these brief and sudden displays of nonsense as well as anyone ever has. He inserts them with the straight-faced accuracy that only masterful comedians have. His whimsical deadpan reminds one of Buster Keaton, Charlie Chaplin, Jack Benny, and also of Mozart when he toys with a brilliant musical idea for a short while but then throws it aside for no reason and in a casual demonstration of genial nonchalance, knowing that he can always draw upon an endless supply within himself.

At times Sturges's playfulness astounds us. For instance, in a scene in *Sullivan's Travels* when the wandering director and his girlfriend are walking alone at night through a wooded area next to a lake, we detect in the semidarkness the lower torso of someone in trousers dangling from the branch of a tree. The two characters do not notice anything and the figure has no place in the narrative. Unless Sturges is commenting on the fact that the poor sometimes hang themselves that way, a reading that seems most unlikely, the shot can only be taken as another example of his cinematic clowning. Since the scene occurs during the heavier segment of the movie, he may have wanted to lighten things up a bit in that place. He may also have been reminding us that, in its entirety, the film is still a comedy. Or even, as Hitchcock farcically told his actors on several occasions, Sturges may have been saying to the audience: "It's *only* a movie."

Throughout his rapid delivery, however, Sturges himself works wonders in his chosen mode of cinematic mythmaking. He is not an illusionist or deceiver, but he does expect his audience to accept the artificial contrivances of his plot. When Harry draws from his vest or sleeve not just a single card or two but entire handfuls, we know that this is an empirical impossibility. The same is true of his tearing up into little pieces Charles's check but later on showing it crumpled but obviously never having been torn at all. Far from feeling cheated, we are delighted by these amusing elements of the plot. They bespeak innovation that is native to the visual and auditory pleasure that Sturges has created for our entertainment as only a masterful artist can.

As another example, I want to consider again the sequence on the train. After Charles has been struck on the head by another falling object—this time, a piece of luggage dropping off its rack—Jean / Eve assaults him with a fictitious account of her previous sex life. She realizes how seriously he will take this, despite the incredulity of what she says. She knows he has not digested her earlier message about good and bad girls, and so he still cannot believe that the bad ones (those who indulge in casual promiscuity, as she alleges about herself in years gone by) are not as bad as he thinks they are. Once more, he swallows the poisoned bait and chokes on it. While this happens inside the train, a furious tempest is battering it on the outside.

White streaks of fake lightning fill the screen, the train shrieks as it runs down the rails, and the orchestral soundtrack articulates a hilarious pastiche of first dramatic but finally histrionic opera music (without the singers but including direct quotes from the repertoire).[8] There is only one way to interpret this marvelous burlesque. In addition to expressing the turmoil that Charles is going through, the sight of most of which we are mercifully spared, it gives Sturges a free and unbridled opportunity to poke fun at the venting of extreme emotionality in some ghastly melodramas of the silent film era.

I suggest that we take all the oddness and inspired irrelevancy in the Sturges movies at their face value, as the jocular and otherwise pointless fooling around through which he presents himself with gusto and bravura. At the same time, what he shows usually serves a purpose in the plot. While the train is speeding across the screen, he inserts a placard on a post outside that instructs the travelers that they are about to go through a tunnel and should pull in their heads. The advice seems whimsical, as it is, until we remember that the axe is now falling on the neck of the turkey Charles.

I see no reason to think that the wild events and extraneous characters in these films are there as a type of Hollywood in-joke about extras or the other appurtenances of moviemaking, as Keane says in agreement with Cavell's notions about cinematic self-reflexivity. That mode of interpretation seems to me unneeded and far-fetched.

❂

This is not to deny that Sturges employs in-jokes at times, as when Muggsy transforms the name *Houdini* into *Whodunit*. A more characteristic display of Sturges's comic talent occurs, however, in the *Lady Eve* scene featuring the horse. In a sequence that is parallel to the one in which Jean observes through her hand mirror what happens behind her head, Eve foretells with almost perfect accuracy what we will be seeing next as her recital dissolves into shots of Charles and herself riding on their horses in a lovely woodland with a waterfall and all the trimmings of storybook romance. As they look out over a beautiful sunset that is clearly meant to be taken as parodistic, Charles repeats the amatory drivel that he used with Jean on the ship in the moonlight.

Eve is able to predict all this because she can read his mind, and because he doesn't recognize her as Jean. Only in one detail does she err, though very slightly. She says that both Charles and the horse will nuzzle her hair. In a private pleasantry with us, Sturges arranges it so that Charles does briefly nuzzle Eve, but she thinks it is the horse and says "Stop that!" This adds a bit of finesse to the repeated nuzzling that Charles's horse then bestows upon the back of *his* head while he persists in delivering the same inane speech we've already heard. Over and over again, the horse intrudes upon it by its annoying though affectionate gesture.

Standing behind Charles, the horse unrelentingly musses up his hair and has to be pushed aside each time. The scene ends with Charles awkwardly embracing Eve with one arm while the other holds back the horse, who whinnies in defeat. The sound it makes is reminiscent of what we heard at the very beginning of the film, when Muggsy tells the native girl he is ditching that he'll send her a postcard. At that time the sound was not a whinnying but a sardonic screeching of jungle noises. Since there are no animals to be seen, we surmise that the filmmaker is giving the horse laugh at Muggsy's egregious suggestion. In the scene that shows Charles getting his hair disordered, we must experience what the horse does as well as the noise it makes as a similar, and equally derisive, commentary that Sturges is himself asserting in response to the gushy nonsense.

Possibly we in the audience should just revel in the hilarity and frivolity in this spectacle of romantic foolishness, on the part of the horse as well as Charles. At the same time, the sequence also replicates the close encounter between Jean and Charles in her stateroom toward the beginning of the film. She led him into a position next to her on a chaise longue, from which he half-falls to the floor in a posture that allows her to press her cheek against his. Aware that his libidinal temperature is soaring in reaction to this contact with her body, she accentuates the suggestive foreplay by delicately fondly his hair and stroking his ear while they converse. That happens shortly after she has tantalized him in the dining room by saying they should go to bed. At the end of the scene, the lengthy lovemaking having led to nothing further, she dismisses him and says she can sleep peacefully now. He staggers off, disgruntled and frustrated, emitting words—"I wish I could say the same"—that make her smile inwardly.

This scene balances the one with the horse not only because of the mussing of Charles's hair but also because of what Jean says on this earlier occasion while administering tactile stimulation. She tells Charles of her girlish dream of giving herself passionately to some stranger who will pounce upon her like a thief in the night. She is teasing Charles. He knows all too well that he himself is far from being impulsive in that way, or impetuous about anything else. To top it all, she mentions that on the enchanted evening in her reverie the air will be filled with the kind of perfume she wears that has almost caused Charles to faint. Since Jean's speech is as comical as Charles's corny protestation of love later on, though also indicative of the hidden longing that simmers in them both, we can take the horse's intervention as a continuation of Jean's wise comments about Charles's inability to understand women, both the good ones and the bad. You can't really believe what you're saying, the horse seems to be telling Charles, and since we too have the same misgivings, we laugh at this unexpected corroboration.

Consequently, I see the horse as a creature in nature who represents Sturges not only as the scriptwriter and director of this movie, but also as someone who applauds Jean/Eve's attempt to knock some horse sense into Charles. The horse's benign nuzzling demonstrates a kind of love that does not issue from the stock language of romantic verbiage. Instead it comes directly out of more organic ingredients of animal life and sensibility. At the same time, the horse is pushy and demanding, competitively intruding him- or herself as a rival object of attention. By the end of the film, but not before, we appreciate the extent to which Charles and Jean/Eve can attain a type of love between them that outdoes whatever this or any other horse may possibly experience in relation to human beings.

This final resolution is predicated upon the forgiveness that Jean bestows upon Charles and that he accords to her, as she had always hoped he would. Eve remains unforgiven, but then she represents the unscrupulous part of herself that Jean had wanted to eradicate. In his terminal statement, which Charles utters as a testament of the capacity to love completely that

Jean has now elicited from him, he insists he doesn't want to learn about her secret life in the past: "Whatever it is, keep it to yourself. All I know is I adore you."

In thus surmounting the pretentious burden of the knowledge of good and evil, inherited from our Judeo-Christian mythology in the West, Charles has finished his course of education and is ready to walk out of Eden hand in hand with this other self. What remains to be seen, when romantic love turns into daily matrimony, is whether Jean will regret her changed condition and revert to being Eve. At that point, we will have reached Sturges's sequel in *The Palm Beach Story*. At its beginning, and then again at the end, a card that flashes on the screen reads: *"And they lived happily ever after . . . or did they?"* But that's another story. And so is *Sullivan's Travels*, which gives the favored, and creatively questing, male a chance to air his side of things.

In *Sullivan's Travels*, released the same year as *The Lady Eve*, the filmmaker protagonist returns from his venture into the heart of social darkness and degradation with a totally different conception of the movie he really wants to make. Instead of being a melodrama called *O Brother, Where Art Thou?*, it will be a comedy that celebrates the grandeur of laughter. We are not told what the new title will be, but we may readily surmise that it could be *Sullivan's Travels*, the movie we have just been watching. Both fictional movies and the one we have actually seen are reborn in the recent film by the Coen brothers, a country music version of Odysseus's mythic travels that is a comedy and not a melodrama but also entitled *O Brother, Where Art Thou?*

With respect to the Sturges movies, the basic motive of *Sullivan's Travels* can be perceived as having established itself better in *The Lady Eve*. Without any social or political aspirations, that film is singleminded in a way that *Sullivan's Travels* is not. Various critics have pointed out that the latter is a strange conglomeration of screwball comedy, melodrama, thriller, and even film noir. On first viewing, one might be confused, as I was, and also annoyed, by the odd clustering of these divergent genres. After several viewings, however, I gradually began to see how well the cinematic styles are joined and interlaced. Where *The Lady Eve* has a single linear progression divided into three parts, like acts in a play, *Sullivan's Travels* is aesthetically much more elaborate. It is self-referential to its multiple being as a film, not because of obscure ontological questions about appearance and reality or the alleged primacy of the visual, but only because it presupposes that its likely audience will have had some acquaintance with the varied types of movies that it yokes together. That gives *Sullivan's Travels* a special tincture that *The Lady Eve* does not have.

In addition, there is another reason why those films differ. *Sullivan's Travels* is an enactment of the myth of the male hero, who finds himself and gains the world only after a journey into the unknown. Several years later Sturges returns to this myth in *Unfaithfully Yours*, which also mingles farcical comedy (indeed extensive slapstick) with the drama of a murder mystery. In it the Rex Harrison character, the greatest of orchestra conductors, struggles to overcome his uncontrollable jealous feelings about a wife who loves him. A related theme appears—with a very different ending and without the comic components—in the much later Ullmann / Bergman film *Faithless*, where the jealous husband is likewise a highly celebrated conductor. Though we first see Jean/Eve on an ocean voyage of conquest and self-discovery, her film is unlike these three. In it the protagonist is a woman who is securely rooted in the affective values of her nature and therefore has no need for a journey that results from inflated aspirations of a male.

In the orthodox myths of the West, women were usually considered to belong to one of two types: they were either good or bad but rarely both. Hebrew mythology distinguished sharply between the Eve who was innocent at first and Lilith, a prior and totally venomous earth force. In Christianity there was Mary Magdalene in contrast to Mary the mother of Christ. Through his fable of Jean/Eve, Sturges demonstrates how both kinds are really one and the same.

Still not all females are identical with his fair lady. The myth of Pygmalion and Galatea, to which I turn next, explores another possibility.

2

Pygmalion Variations

In Ovid's telling of the Pygmalion myth, we do not learn much about Galatea. She is the figurine that Pygmalion has created as a statue, and that Venus then brings to life as a woman. In a recent free rendition of *The Metamorphoses*, we read that once the maiden has attained consciousness, "she blinks, blushes, opens her eyes, and gazes upon him, / her maker, her lover, her man, and behind him the light of the sky, / for which she is grateful to him and the goddess."[1] The lovers instantly consummate their union, and Venus arranges for a child to emerge from that. It is called Paphos, which then becomes the name of a place that is sacred to Venus. Ovid tells us nothing further about Galatea or the nature of Pygmalion's love for her. The story's function as mythology is complete without such information.

In most later versions of the myth, Galatea's personhood receives scarcely more attention. In eighteenth-century cartoons, she is even presented as merely a sex object, a succulent artifact of explicit pornography designed to give pleasure to men and to arouse sexual ardor in women. George Bernard Shaw alters this aspect of the myth completely. Though the title of his play makes reference to only the man who turns a flower girl into a lady, Shaw is largely concerned with probing her eventual liberation as it interacts with the creativity of her up-to-date Pygmalion. That is especially true of his play's film version, for which Shaw was the principal screenwriter. Moreover, in the cinematic transcription of *My Fair Lady,* Lerner and Lowe's musical treatment of both the play and the film, the Galatea surrogate stands out as the character with whom spectators are expected to identify regardless of their gender.

Coherent with its derivation from a myth, the classic movie directed by Anthony Asquith and Leslie Howard, and produced by Gabriel Pascal, presents Eliza Doolittle as a young woman who lives in the past as well as the present. Though her story takes place just before World War II, as indicated by the style of clothing and the vintage of the automobiles, she embodies dilemmas of the "new woman" that had begun to appear in the last quarter of the nineteenth century. When he wrote the play in 1915, and then the movie script in 1938, Shaw capitalized on the fact that those dilemmas were still prevalent in the Anglo-Saxon world. The global success of *My Fair Lady* attests to their continuing importance in other cultures as well. Like *The Lady Eve,* both the musical and the earlier film explore a facet of modern femininity that I touched on in the previous chapter and can now investigate more fully.

I am referring to the need, in Eliza Doolittle as in Jean Harrington, to *remake* her womanhood, to turn herself into a new woman. Jean finally succeeds in that attempt, but only after acting like the virulent Eve she does not want to be. As if by magic, though actually by force of will, Eliza sloughs off her former state. This is the white magic of self-love in contrast to the black magic to which Jean/Eve resorts throughout her attempt to attain what she wished to be by ensnaring someone else's love. But Eliza, too, can reach a final solution only after she goes through a dark night of the soul. Having won her creator's bet, as Job does in winning God's wager with the devil, Eliza discovers to her horror that she does not know what kind of life she is now fit to live. (Indeed, the happy ending to the biblical story—Job being blissfully replenished with the new children that God has given to him in recompense for the ones that have been destroyed—is so implausible as to make us doubt that he could ever have gained an exemplary existence in view of what he has suffered.)

Eliza eventually survives her crisis. Like Jean/Eve, she is a born survivor who deep down remains positively the same dame. In the process of finding herself as she truly is, she becomes one of the great mythic figures of the age. The myth that she dominates is not only a reenactment of Adam and Eve's but also a variant of it. Despite the assistance that Henry Higgins provides, the new woman that Eliza becomes is someone who recreates herself in the process of digesting the fruit of phonetic knowledge. Jean/Eve Harrington had only to cleanse her criminal inclinations, and through her love of Charles she manages to do that, but Eliza Doolittle changes so completely that even a fellow flower girl cannot recognize her at the end. In relating this self-creation, the Shavian fable moves beyond the story of Adam and Eve and even opens to inspection contemporary questions about the gender of the being who created everything in general.

As represented in Genesis, God is obviously a male, a loving but also severe father figure. Through the élan vital that enables her to become a lady, not just to *act* like one as Lady Eve does, Eliza makes us wonder whether the ultimate progenitor of reality might not be a kindred female demiurge. Repeatedly insisting that he has turned a squashed cabbage leaf into a lady, on the model of God molding Adam out of earth, Higgins arrogates to himself the divine spark that explains Eliza's transformation. But in its totality, the plot reveals that something very deep in Eliza accounts for this miraculous occurrence. She has subtly put Higgins's expertise to use as a vehicle to her destiny as an autonomous individual. Though he gravitates about her in a correlative myth of his own, he is not the equivalent of the Ovidian Venus who brings to life the marmoreal statue Pygmalion has carved. Eliza alone has accomplished that, in an immaculate conception of herself for which Higgins was a convenient intermediary.

In his stage production, and even more so in the subsequent movie, Shaw turns everything topsy-turvy as he did in so many other dramatic vehicles. A dustman is awarded wealth, and separately and for the better his daughter alters her station in class-ridden England. Not only is Shaw's new woman Galatea given equal, or greater, importance than the proficient professor in scene after scene, but also her counterweight is not a free-ranging artist or devotee of the goddess of love and beauty. He is instead a scholar and technician, a specialist in linguistics.

Though Higgins sculpts Eliza in the manner of a talented teacher, he never begs any Venus to satisfy the amatory inclinations he might have in relation to this perfectable woman. He prides himself on always being emotionally correct, purely professional, with her as he is with all his other pupils. Sexual passion is for him, as for most of the Shavian heroes, inferior to intellectual passions that permeate his mind. Higgins has immersed himself in the realm of ideas. He is above all a thinker, and not at all a philanderer. On the other hand, he is often, and comically, shown to be out of touch with social reality and innocently mistaken about his own feelings and behavior. Before discussing that, however, we should focus on something Shaw says about Eliza in his long epilogue.

Explaining why, after the curtain has come down, Eliza will not marry Higgins, Shaw remarks:

> She is immensely interested in him. She has even secret mischievous moments in which she wishes she could get him alone, on a desert island, away from all ties and with nobody else in the world to consider, and just drag him off his pedestal and see him making love like any common man. We all have private imaginations of that sort. But when it comes to business, to the life that she really leads as distinguished from the life of dreams and fancies, she likes Freddy [the nonentity who adores her throughout the play] and she likes the Colonel [courtly Pickering, who invariably treats her like a lady]; and she does not like Higgins and Mr. Doolittle [her father, Alfred Doolittle]. Galatea never does quite like Pygmalion: his relation to her is too godlike to be altogether agreeable.[2]

Note that it is not Shaw's Galatea who stands on a pedestal. His donnish Pygmalion does. Though in the Shavian presentation, as in Ovid's, Pygmalion is "immensely interested" in his Galatea, as she is in him, the nature of Higgins's interest is totally different from Eliza's. The Ovidian sculptor was enamored of his statue as any man might feel toward a beautiful woman who evokes a passionate sexual desire and then satisfies it happily. While Shaw's Galatea can be thought to have libidinal feelings for her tutor, there is no reason to believe that Higgins experiences anything comparable toward her. He is an "old [meaning inveterate] bachelor," as he calls himself early on, whose erotic disposition—whatever it may be: heterosexual, homosexual, or possibly neither—does not change very much from the first to the last act.

Like someone who has read Ovid's *The Art of Love*, the original Greek or Latin Pygmalion worships the exquisite statue as if her embodiment of the ideal he has always sought puts her in the same category as Venus. He even makes gift offerings to the marble icon and bestows upon her luxuries—playthings and soft pillows, for instance—that might encourage a real, living, girl to yield to his carnal impulse. In one recounting of the myth, Pygmalion is said to have created the statue after his sexual overtures had been directed to Venus but rejected by her. Only later does she compensate him by graciously giving life to the statue that bears a clear resemblance to herself. Shaw's Pygmalion has feelings that are neither amatory nor overtly sexual. He delights in his ability to help Eliza emancipate herself, and even after she proclaims her declaration of independence, he glories in the fact that his grand achievement among women has become a "consort battleship."

My Fair Lady is radically different. By the time it was written in 1956 (film release, 1964), Shaw was dead, and his hostility toward romanticism was submerged by the idealization of sexual pairing out of which popular musicals were still being made on the stage and in the movies. But even the earlier film had reached beyond Shaw's original design. It ends with Eliza returning to the house on Wimpole Street and renewing her previous place in it. Higgins cocks his hat, swivels in his chair so that only his back is visible, and speaks into the empty air the words that formerly provoked her outburst when they and Colonel Pickering returned from her triumph at the ball. As if nothing new has happened, he intones with absolute assurance: "Where the devil are my slippers, Eliza?" The instructions for the soundtrack script then read as follows: "As the ballroom theme swells into a crescendo, a fade-out from the back of Higgins's head. The lilting music of the ballroom waltz is heard as 'The End' and the cast are flashed upon the screen."[3]

This ending, fully conveyed in the Arthur Honegger score, leaves open the idea that Eliza might indeed be or become a consort battleship for Higgins. But as yet she still remains an underling.

When the premiere of the film turned out to be an enormous success, Shaw was asked why he had apparently abandoned his staunchly anti-Romantic stance. He brushed aside the question, saying that the modifications of his play were "too inconclusive to be worth making a fuss about."[4] In earlier years Shaw had refused to allow any filming of his works that would differ in the slightest from their prior stage production. The two movies that accommodated this demand, *Arms and the Man* and *How He Lied to Her Husband*, were dismal failures both critically and commercially. Being reproductions of what occurs in the theater, they showed little understanding of the opportunities afforded by cinematic art. The greatness of the *Pygmalion* film results, in large degree, from its exceptional ability to exploit these aesthetic opportunities.

We could possibly explain the transmutation of Shaw's play by inferring that he had fallen under the influence of the wily producer Pascal, or that in his eighties he was mentally ill-equipped to oppose the romanticization of his former ideas, or even that he was succumbing to the hope of enormous profits that accompany popular acclaim by moviegoers. But in relation to each of these possibilities, the situation was always more complicated. Delighted with Pascal as he was at first, Shaw criticized his judgment and his procedure on many occasions during production. Moreover, Shaw had minutely supervised the last version of the screenplay himself. He appears in the credits as the principal scenarist, and he received the Oscar that year in his own name. His being over eighty seems wholly irrelevant. Finally, there lurks a residual truth in the famous anecdote about Shaw's earlier negotiations with Sam Goldwyn and what he said in terminating them: "The trouble with you, Mr. Goldwyn, is that you're interested only in art; while I'm interested only in money."[5] The financial lure was nothing new to Shaw.

In his book *The Serpent's Eye: Shaw and the Cinema*, Donald P. Costello traces Shaw's theories, over a period of thirty-two years, about the nature of movies as well as his active participation in the filming of his plays. Costello concludes that "Shaw, fascinated as he was by the movies, was a good movie writer to the degree that he departed from his own philosophy of the cinema, to the degree, that is, that his cinema practice contradicted his cinema theory."[6] As a generalization about Shaw's involvement with moviemaking, this statement may be taken as more or less correct. But its basic insight has to be placed within a broader conception of Shavian thought.

In the early days, when Shaw refused to allow on-screen more than a duplication of what he had written for the stage, he was resisting the elimination or shortening of long speeches he had given his characters. These speeches were declamations of the various ideas proffered in each play. To the extent that the concepts are vividly articulated and amply suggestive, they lend themselves to dramatic as well as polemical investigation. In Shaw's use of them, the theater becomes a lecture hall as well as a source of entertainment. Shaw feared that the talkiness included in all his plays, and required by his most dialectical ones, would be excised, or worse yet, trivialized in cinematic renditions geared to some massive populace that brings only its ready cash to a performance. In the case of *Pygmalion*, however, he must have felt that it required so little talkiness, so little discursive exposition, that a truly filmic version could work as an authentic companion to what he had put on stage and later enriched by his printed preface and afterword.

If this is true, we should be able to show why the *Pygmalion* film works as well as it does, and also why it is authentic Shavian mythmaking in ways that are also native to cinematic art in general. Consider the second act in which Eliza's transformation begins. The clothes in which she arrived have been burned and she herself has been bathed, indeed scrubbed, by Mrs. Pearce, the majordomo of the Higgins household. In the movie we have already seen a montage of Higgins wrapped in a dressing gown that makes him look like a magician, a wonder-worker who may very well be capable of turning "this guttersnipe" into a lady, as he says once he has decided to accept Pickering's wager. His facial expression then was intense and maniacal, as if he might even be a mad scientist capable of inadvertently making the flower girl into a Frankensteinian monster. But after the scene with Eliza's father, and after Eliza has returned cleaned and combed and swaddled in a floral Chinese dressing gown, his concentrated features appear in a montage similar to the first one except that now he seems quite sane and businesslike as he shrewdly studies Eliza while mapping out the project that lies before them both.

At this moment in the narrative, Shaw had interrupted the play and inserted a prose passage that begins: "There seems to be some curiosity as to what Higgins's lessons to Eliza were like. Well, here is a sample."[7] He then resorts to dialogue that might occur onstage and formulates a scene in which Eliza painfully learns how to replace her lower-class vowels with others that are more genteel. At the end she runs sobbing from the room. The curtain then comes down on the second act. When it rises again, we are in the drawing room of Higgins's mother. Eliza's development has reached a point where Higgins and Pickering feel that they can try her out in a small and semi-formal gathering. In the movie there is a filmed transition to this event that occurs between the second and third acts. It shows in much greater detail than the passage Shaw had written what constitutes Eliza's training in phonetics and polite decorum.

This cinematic interlude takes about five minutes, a significant chunk of time in either a movie or a play. With few words being spoken by anyone, it packs a vast amount of information into a rapid cluster of images that satisfy our curiosity about Eliza's preparation. The speed of the cutting not only keeps our visual imagination at its sharpest edge but also suggests, with an economy of means, the fact that the tutoring we observe has taken weeks and even months. The more our engrossed perception moves quickly from one shot to the next, the more we sense the lengthiness of the depicted process in its entirety. The mere succession of these montages articulates, better than any verbal description could, the details and temporal duration of Eliza's educational experience.

By the time the *Pygmalion* movie was made, audiences had long since learned how to appreciate the extensive meaningfulness in the techniques being used for this purpose—the dissolves, close-ups, artificial angles or filters of the camera, and the different music from moment to moment. Many theorists, then and now, have considered these devices distinctively "cinematic," definitive of film media as such. Without questioning that belief in this place, I want to show that by studying the *use* of these contrivances we may help explain the mythmaking capacity that is native to the art form.

In all myths the human experience of time is changed in order to enable a trained and sympathetic audience to transcend its ordinary sense of past, present, and future as they exist in their usual linear progression. The rubric "once upon a time," which is characteristic of mythmaking, itself abstracts us from the parameters of our habitual life from day to day. The term signifies a non-historic time, not before recorded history but *outside* it and exceeding our normal existence by giving us an aesthetic leverage upon it. The "once" does not connote a particular moment, but rather some occurrence that is momentous. In movies this modus operandi is carried out by the techniques that both formulate and project the meaning of each ingredient image.

After the shot of Higgins's prolonged stare as he sizes up his new pupil, the relevant segment in the film begins by displaying the arm of a turntable as it descends upon a recording. While the agitated music accentuates our feeling that a somewhat frantic activity is underway, we see Higgins pointing to a chart about places in the mouth from which vowel sounds originate. Eliza watches closely but then immediately afterward we see her, in her nightclothes and in bed, moving her head back and forth on the pillow while she is asleep. The accompanying music consists of eerie sounds appropriate to fitful dreaming. Next, in his parlor somewhat later, Higgins instructs Eliza in her pronunciation. He is in a coat and tie, but she is dressed in the sweater and hair band that identify her as a schoolgirl. Another shot of her asleep and tossing in bed follows, the music becoming isomorphically more insistent and anxious-sounding.

Thereafter Higgins pops into Eliza's mouth several marbles, one of which she swallows to her horror. Higgins takes no interest in her consternation and coolly remarks that he has plenty more. The recording then turns rhythmically on its platter as the music makes noises reminiscent of a carnival merry-go-round. Higgins's head suddenly appears superimposed on the horn of his antique phonograph. Another scene of nerve-racking instruction ensues, after which Eliza is in bed again, and then we see montages of dressmakers, beauticians, and others who assist in Higgins's creativity. Wearing street clothes that suggest a more advanced stage of training, in contrast to her school uniform, Eliza shows progress in the various social skills she has been acquiring. Finally, once this visual documentation about the transforming of a guttersnipe has been completed, Higgins and Pickering agree that Eliza is ready for her trial run at Mrs. Higgins's home day.

Eliza having failed to pass muster on that occasion, Higgins increases the fervor of his instruction. In scenes similar to the ones I have just described, the cascading montages fade into each other and become even more frenetic than before. At times Honegger's music seems to throw up its hands in despair or fatigue. Both of these sequences were written for the film production and are thoroughly cinematic inasmuch as no other art can approximate the effect they evoke. It is not only a convergence of different events in ordinary life, but also a combination of them into bundles of perceptual elements that belong only to motion pictures. In its totality each bundle expresses, as opposed to merely representing, bits of human experience that register very quickly in our awareness despite their being abstractions out of the reality we know directly.

After the second of these sequences, we are immediately launched into the Embassy ball portion of the film. It takes up almost eleven minutes and replaces the garden party, not seen but only mentioned in the play as the setting of Eliza's great triumph. With merely scarce and scattered dialogue, the filmed version is presented as grandiose spectacle interwoven with narrative suspense throughout. We are regaled with the sight of aristocratic-looking people, the men in evening clothes and the women gorgeously attired, all of them acting with studied nobility in the sumptuous splendor of a London palace, while the protagonists bravely confront the frightening possibility that Eliza will be recognized as a fraud. Once she excels in her charade, the plot returns to the same thematic texture as the play. The mythic content of this story about the fabrication of social importance and elegance in a lower-class person then receives its denouement in the culminating resolution between the modern Galatea and her contemporary Pygmalion. I will turn to that presently, but first I want to continue my speculations about the nature and significance of mythmaking in film.

I have been suggesting that while movies like *Pygmalion* can and do manifest their mythological function in words and action that may differ only slightly from what exists onstage in a theater, or in the pages of a novel, cinematic techniques such as the ones that propel the two sequences I described, and the splendid spectacle that imbues the ballroom segment, are themselves *inherently* mythical. They lull us into an acceptance of idealized eventualities, though seemingly realistic and often negated by the harsh circumstances that delimit our life in nature. This property of film art induces a suspension of disbelief by repudiating the routine order of things to which we are accustomed. However much the moving images retain an indubitable semblance to reality, what they present is not *real*, but only, at its best, *true*.

The real world is continuous and consecutive, and often baffling. It is not cut up in a string of montages neatly ordered and subtly devised to communicate artificial and preconceived meanings that may nevertheless penetrate into the substance of what is neither artificial nor preconceived. The construction of this aesthetic truthfulness sustains the mythic impulse. While telling a beguiling story, films like *Pygmalion* marshal ocular effects carefully chosen from the real world. They thereby create mythological visions that can be deeply philosophical in their persistent probing.

Above all in *Pygmalion* as it was filmed, the miraculous compression of months into a few minutes of strictly integrated shots makes us wonder how greatly human relations—in the feelings between men and women, for instance—may be understood in a comparable manner. Is it possible that these attachments we all endure are really disjointed, though perhaps unifiable, sentiments that only a work of art can truly explicate (as Proust believed)? In the beginning Higgins had remarked that, when the experiment was done, Eliza could be thrown back in the gutter to fend for herself as she had before. He refused to consider that she might "have feelings." We laugh at her vehement insistence that she does, as well as at his blatant arrogance in denying that she could. At the end they have both learned something about the nature of feeling. Once she has acquired an adequate voice for asserting what she feels, they each come to realize how volatile and chaotic all feelings are—in him as well as her.

Presenting this mutual discovery through the vivacity of its flickering images and startling shots, the film imparts a panoramic message about our sheer existence. It does so within a fanciful tale, as in other myths. Remaining close to our affective being in a work of make-believe, instead of didactic or prosaic philosophy, the movie fulfills the promise of the play's subtitle: "a romance in five acts." No actual romance occurs in five acts. That is an arbitrary convention of the theater. By invoking the supervening modes of representation that cinematic art affords, the movie *Pygmalion* acquires an augmented purchase upon the erotic realities that Shaw wished to depict and also transcend. What, then, does it tell us about those realities, and how do its insights comport with the rest of Shavian teaching?

Shaw's subtitle prepares us for the contents, as well as the formal pattern, of his mythological effort. Offering themselves as a romance, both movie and play establish their origin in, as well as their alienation from, the great tradition of Romantic literature that delineates an everlasting bond that unites exceptional men and women. Shaw implies that what he portrays in the five acts onstage, or their employment in the film, will not last beyond the boundaries of the narrative. And indeed the printed version of the play's epilogue is explicitly anti-Romantic in its portrayal of what happens once the final curtain comes down.

Even so, the story in the play, the film, and the musical alike gravitates about a relationship that mimics typical romances in Western mythology. As in the Tristan myth, it begins with hostility between male and female which transitions into their mutual struggle within a challenging situation posed by external forces. Their alliance then culminates in a viable oneness between them. Shaw tailors this pliable material as the unfolding of a close and ongoing relationship between a scholarly man and a flower girl. Aloof or even inimical as these two would normally be, they create between them an ambitious project, work hard to carry it out, and finally cap their victory with a recognition of their limited need for each other in the future.

Having conformed to this extent, Shaw explicitly rejects the usual outcome. The resolution in that type of plot derives from adherence to social mandates about love and marriage. In the Romantic tradition, the idealized protagonists either die for having thwarted current mores or else become a married couple who live happily ever after, as if to affirm that proper matrimony was what they really wanted all along. Sometimes, as in Shakespeare's *Much Ado About Nothing*, they may justify the connubial conclusion by arguing that the world must be peopled. But whether or not the lovers have a reasonable belief of that sort, we know they behave as they finally do because it is what their society, represented by us in the audience, expects of them.

Shaw repudiates any such expectation. His Pygmalion makes a lady out of a squashed cabbage leaf as a means of changing society itself. When Eliza berates him for not behaving like Pickering, who treats a flower girl as if she were a duchess, Higgins replies: "And I treat a duchess as if she was a flower girl." This is a revolutionary principle. It undermines the status quo and furthers the idea of a utopian order in which everyone is treated alike. As Higgins says in justifying the enterprise of creating a new way of speaking for Eliza: "It's filling up the deepest gulf that separates class from class and soul from soul."

The Romantic ideology that Shaw was attacking runs counter to these statements of Higgins. It ordains special privilege for the one and only person with whom each lover pledges to share his or her innermost being. In none of the versions of Shaw's *Pygmalion* do Higgins and Eliza get married. When Wendy Hiller, in the movie of the play, and Audrey Hepburn, in the movie of the musical, return to Higgins and presumably accept their former situation in his house, they manifest the visage of cheerful acquiescence. That alone eliminates the conflict between male and female, and projects their future collaboration together. But it does not amount to a matrimonial commitment that will issue into the kind of glorified institution that Romantic literature envisions.

All the same, the concluding moments of the movie versions do greatly modify the defiant import of Higgins's final outburst on stage. In the last moment of the original play, he roars with laughter after exclaiming: "She's going to marry Freddy. Ha, ha! Freddy! Freddy! Ha ha ha ha ha!!!!!"[8] Earlier in the scene, he confessed to Eliza that he had grown accustomed to her voice and appearance. He says this not because he is in love, but rather as a plausible indication of his friendly concern about her. When she indignantly replies that, without any assistance from him, she will earn her living by teaching others the phonetic skills she has now mastered, he compliments her on being "a tower of strength."

None of this comes even close to the ending of *My Fair Lady* in which Higgins sings an arietta, not unlike a lover's, about his having reluctantly become used to Eliza: "Her joys, her woes, her highs, her lows are second nature to me now, like breathing out and breathing in." His poignant lament terminates with the admission that he has "become accustomed to the trace of something in the air, accustomed to her face." We recognize this painful alternation of feelings for and against his attraction to Eliza as the agonized sign of love he cannot control.

When Eliza comes back to Higgins in the musical, she reads the same lines that occur in the Pascal movie but then, as enacted by Audrey Hepburn, she smiles appealingly and steps forward with accommodating steps that signify her kindliness and warmth toward him in his depressed condition. Her gratuitous gesture must be interpreted as expressive of more than just good will on her part. It bespeaks the female's acceptance of her amorous role. The condition is underlined and ratified by the extended music that began with Higgins's intonation of his feelings and now swells with the appearance of forgiving and compliant Eliza. It is lush and gently lilting music, played effusively by the strings, somewhat sentimental but also entirely appropriate to the erotic amplitude in romanticized emotion.

The last scene of the Pascal film is positioned between the play and the musical. In both film and play, the dynamic in the exchange between Higgins and Eliza is largely composed of his response to her suggestions about her future prospects. When she says she will become an assistant to his Hungarian pupil Nepommuck (renamed Karpathy in the film), Higgins smolders with annoyance at her treachery; when she insists that she will teach what she has learned from him, he laughs contemptuously at her presumption; when she tells him she will marry Freddy, he explodes in anger. It is not jealousy or male competitiveness that evokes his furor. It is the very idea that his supreme creation should be wasted on a nobody, as he rightly takes Freddy to be.

Much earlier, when Eliza has her initial tryout at his mother's tea, Higgins had already shown his view of Freddy by absentmindedly using the young man's outstretched hand as a hat rack. In finding her voice, Eliza attacks Higgins as a cruel and selfish tyrant, but what has driven him throughout is the idealistic desire to make a superlative product—in this case, a companion for kings rather than for someone like Freddy—whose adulation only proves his abject worthlessness. In the vehemence of the five exclamation marks that encapsulate the voluminous laugh in his final speech, Higgins appears at last as a wildly passionate artist who now perceives the hideous possibility that his greatest achievement may be ruined or misused.

In the very beginning of the film, we see Higgins wandering by himself across a deserted Covent Garden as he searches for phonetic raw material that he copies into his notebook. He comes upon a couple of porters conversing in their dialect and writes down their words in shorthand. When members of the opera audience and other people gather in the portico of the church to escape the pouring rain, he is likewise the solitary observer who says nothing and coolly writes on, as if he were taking dictation from the mouth of life itself. In his exchanges with the flower girl and her potential clients, he remains apart and composed, though brutal in his remarks to Eliza and slightly annoyed when a bystander intimates that he must have escaped from an insane asylum.

It is only as his work with Eliza advances that we perceive how intensely dedicated Higgins really is. He has the cognitive passion that Shaw extols in various writings. By the end of the film, this intellectual man discovers powerful forces in himself that are not at all rational. His development in this regard intersects with the mental growth that Eliza undergoes. When she walks out on Higgins, she has reached a point at which she can think and function as cogently as he can. In Wendy Hiller's enactment, Eliza returns as a tolerant and affectionate, but equally competent, coworker who will not fawn excessively over her teacher. Romantic love has no essential place in this newly fashioned relation.

Two conclusions follow from my reading of Pascal's film version. First, it vindicates Shaw's assertion that the ending of his screenplay is "too inconclusive" to fuss over and therefore cannot be taken to mean that he has modified his views about romantic love. But also, it raises questions about the nature of the myth that is purveyed in this movie, and how it pertains to Shaw's view of human attachments as a whole. The key to these mythological implications of *Pygmalion* lies in the concept of "passion."

In all its versions the play is thematically constructed out of the interaction between the two types of passion I have mentioned. From the very outset Eliza Doolittle is not just another flower girl plying her trade in Covent Garden. Having escaped her father and the six "stepmothers" he has forced upon her, she lives alone in proud isolation, inhabiting a slum room with only a bird in its cage as her roommate. In the film she talks to it, as if it were another self whose unnatural constriction symbolizes her own sense of imprisonment. Though she is uneducated and unprepared for any escape into the wider world of open opportunity and social distinction, Eliza is filled with an eagerness to find improvement wherever she can. She bursts upon Higgins's upper-class domain as someone who has the life-enhancing, albeit self-oriented, energies without which the human species could not survive. As in the Romantic mythology she has inherited as a "new woman" at this moment of English culture, she embodies the passionate will to live that Shaw, following Schopenhauer, considered primordial in all of nature.

Eliza brings to the drama the element of sex, and ideally sexual love, that even repressed Romantics sought with religious fervor. That is the background of Pickering's demand to know whether Higgins is a man of honor in his dealings with female pupils. It is not just a matter of Eliza's being a young girl living as a ward in Higgins's home. It is also a sign of Pickering's knowledge that Eliza's passionate nature would make her vulnerable to carnal intrusion on Higgins's part. By the end of this "romance" he, and we, have been disabused of any apprehension of this sort. Though occasionally tempted, Higgins remains faithful to the other type of passion, no less Romantic than Eliza's and not totally unlike hers, yet belonging to another state of spirit that she, as a warm and sprightly person, scarcely understands.

In *Man and Superman*, Shaw calls that latter kind "the mightiest of the passions."[9] *Man and Superman* centers around the premarital ambivalence of a man who wishes to live in the world of thought and political action while also retaining his instinctual desire to marry the eligible woman who pursues him in her own ambivalent manner. Like Shakespeare's Beatrice and Benedick, the two are made for each other despite (and because of) their sexual warfare. They have grown up together in the same social class, and they have both been educated into the matrimonial conventions of their milieu. John Tanner, an imperfect incarnation of Don Juan, flees the allurements of Ann Whitefield out of adherence to the code of bachelorhood that young and idle rich men like himself routinely cherished at the time. When he succumbs to the propriety of marriage, as Benedick does but Don Juan would not have, it is because he thinks the species requires that biological union. Neither he nor Shaw faces up to the fact that each of them also believes that creative evolution can only emanate from the unwavering efforts of the upward-striving intellectual who never marries (or, at least, not for reasons of romantic love).

In *Pygmalion* the principals are not at all made for each other, though their gravitational paths overlap as the narrative progresses. Its mythological content is therefore systematically different from the one that structures *Man and Superman*. As a bachelor who supervises Eliza's miraculous re-creation, Higgins is a substitute father rather than a potential suitor. He and Mr. Doolittle communicate with each other as members of the same generation, though Higgins is obviously younger. They are both what Doolittle calls "men of the world," by which he means men who know how to survive in the world without yielding unduly to hormonal urges that wreak havoc among those who are still immature. In an absurdist gesture, Higgins contrives to elevate the social status of Doolittle, who even allows himself to get married and become a victim of middle-class morality.

But in all this, there is no libidinal romance at stake, and those who suspect a quasi-incestuous intimacy between the teacher and his female tutee simply miss the point. Nevertheless the difference between *Man and Superman* and the filmed *Pygmalion* or *My Fair Lady* is partly distorted by cinematic and musical effects in the latter two that do suggest the *conceivability* of some misalliance between Higgins and Eliza. While marriage, including a marriage of convenience, will not take place between these characters, we in the audience are nudged into a semidaydream that somehow fuses the two kinds of passion into an amorphous bond between them that Shaw considered ludicrous. In that sense the magical aura of these movies remains closer to the Ovidian source than anything Shaw may have wanted.

Attempting in the stage play to draw upon ordinary life in the London of his day, he had no need of either a love goddess or a susceptible sculptor who can carve a beautiful statue that is not only lifelike but also comes alive. In reinterpreting the myth, Shaw wished to modify its meaning by emphasizing the implications in *any* creative exchange between human beings. This did not exclude the utility of the cineastic and musical devices in the movie versions, but it did prevent them from turning the myth into just another vehicle of Romantic theory. As Shaw stated in an early production note: "The producer should bear in mind from the beginning that it is Freddy who captivates and finally carries off Eliza, and that all suggestion of a love interest between Eliza and Higgins should be most carefully avoided."[10]

Hitchcock's *Vertigo* (1958) partakes of the Pygmalion myth in a way that contrasts with the movies based on Shaw's play. Released two years after *My Fair Lady, Vertigo* is a comparable romance enclosed within the style that characterizes most of Hitchcock's work. I have elsewhere analyzed the five elemental modalities that are native to his art: the thriller, the mystery, the whodunit, the suspense film, and the horror movie.[11] The first four serve as integral parts of *Vertigo,* and perhaps the last as well in places—for example, in the shots of Scottie hanging from a gutter at the beginning and of a woman's body falling (twice) from the bell tower later on. In *Vertigo* these tools of Hitchcock's trade are deployed in a story about a partly disabled detective who overcomes his guilt-ridden fear of heights by discovering the truth about a woman with whom he has fallen in love and who really is guilty, though at first he has no knowledge of that. She appears as two women in the fiction: the cool, remote, and ethereal Madeleine and the vibrant, earthy, and lower-class Judy. The second is subjected to Scottie's attempt to transform her into a replica of the first one. His endeavor is similar to Higgins's effort to help Eliza change herself into someone who can pass as upper-class. Higgins's success is permanent; Scottie's is very short-lived.

Apart from this divergence, the two approaches to the Pygmalion myth differ in their overall genre. Suspense does play a role in the Shavian movie, since we must always wonder whether Higgins is capable of doing what he intends, whether Eliza will or will not be unmasked at the Embassy ball, and whether the two principals will stay together after they have won the wager. Nevertheless, there is in *Pygmalion* nothing of the thriller, the mystery, the whodunit, or the horror film. In *Vertigo* these predominate until Judy comes into Scottie's life; thereafter the film is largely given over to the problematics of romance. But though it resembles *My Fair Lady* to that extent, only the Hitchcock movie delves into the psychological ambiguities that pertain to the emotional situation it portrays.

In the first half of *Vertigo*, Scottie spurns the proffered affection of Midge, a likable and attractive former girlfriend who is clearly in love with him. He then becomes intrigued, both professionally and personally, by the strangely alluring Madeleine. She seems to live in the past as a young beauty who died tragically more than a hundred years earlier. Madeleine jumps into San Francisco Bay in a presumed attempt to commit suicide, and then ostensibly falls to her death from the top of the bell tower. The Judy who later appears has—like her name itself—none of the elevated demeanor of Madeleine. In the letter Judy writes to Scottie, she confesses about having playacted Madeleine. When she immediately tears up that letter, we realize that her love for him makes her willing to endure his obsessional need to renew his painful memory of the woman he thinks is dead. Though Judy resists the attempts to make her look and act like her, she yields to his demands because she thinks he may then like her as she is and even love her for herself.

This is more than Eliza in *Pygmalion* could have expected, and toward the end of *Vertigo* Judy's hope is fulfilled only briefly. The validation of her love is presented in a quasi-magical sequence that Hitchcock handles brilliantly. Judy has allowed herself to be clothed in a grey suit similar to the one that Madeleine wore, and she even accepts the dyeing treatment that changes the color of her hair, causing it to resemble Madeleine's. After Scottie insists, she puts up her hair in a small bun as Madeleine used to do. That completes her transformation into the beloved.

Entering the room in which Scottie is waiting for her, Judy slowly walks toward him with the seductive gait that Madeleine had. Hitchcock's cinematographic filter encases her in a smoky haze as if she were emerging from a mysterious and even mystical domain. It is in fact the native miasma of Scottie's pathological infatuation, both a height of ideality that frightens him and an embodiment of his longing for tainted though mutual love as the Romantic tradition portrayed it. In her reciprocating manner, Judy's smile seems to promise a happy outcome. Their fervent embrace and ardent kissing establish a consummatory oneness. Soon after, however, the truth about her identity intervenes and that shatters Scottie's dream. Madeleine/Judy having been proved to be the same and criminal, he can no longer love her in either aspect of her being. Neither the Shavian nor the related versions of the Pygmalion story have a mythic conclusion of that sort.

The implications of Scottie's failure in each of his love experiences are captured in the last shot of *Vertigo*. It shows him standing on the outside ledge of the bell tower, looking down at Judy's lifeless body far below. He is not holding on to anything, which tells us that his fear of heights has now been cured, but his arms are outstretched sideways as if to express his forlorn and wretched condition in having lost the woman he loved despite the anguish she engendered. Scottie had forced Judy up the stairs of the bell tower as the last thing he must do in order to free them both from the past—above all, from the fabricated history of Madeleine. It does free Judy, but only because she dies in the process. Though he himself has been liberated from his physical distress, he is condemned to live with the vertigo of an affective disease that will forever ravage within him.

In displaying Judy's submission to Scottie's attempts to reconstruct her, *Vertigo* (and Chantal Akerman's Proustian film *La Captive* as well) resembles not only *Pygmalion* but also *The Lady Eve*. Jean's decision to con high society by pretending to be a lady has its inspirational source in her previous assertion that out of love for Charles she will make herself into everything he wants her to be. So too we may imagine that Judy wishes to become the character Madeleine that she has created through her inventive impersonation. Loving Scottie as a possible mate, she manifests a desire to emulate the Madeleine kind of cultivation that he finds appealing. As if by magic, she is eager to be *turned into* Madeleine.

In each of the three movies I have discussed, the two female types are played by the same actress. Though Eliza Doolittle has only one name that applies to her before and after her re-creation, she aspires from the start to be in her later self a sophisticated lady that Higgins might admire. They are heroic women who struggle to unify the alternate personas in themselves. Eliza and Jean / Eve do so, more or less. In her fall from grace, Madeleine / Judy cannot. She resembles the two women in Ingmar Bergman's *Persona*, who try to merge their separate personalities but discover the impossibility of that. They merge only in the photographic image of their faces, which in fact makes them both look like monsters.

In *Vertigo* the complexities of the basic motif, with all its mythic overtones, are transmitted not only by the narrative effects but also by the music and the expressionistic artwork, swirling dizzily during the opening credits and then spiraling inwardly and outwardly as if in a stressful dream. Without these technical contributions of the artwork and the music, the rudimentary plot could well have seemed tawdry and superficial. Bernard Herrmann's score is especially interesting because it brings out the operatic dimension of the movie. As with Verdi or Puccini, Herrmann's sonic presence is more than just an accompaniment to what is being seen or spoken by the characters. It also provides its own musical continuity, and even interpretation at various points, particularly during the many minutes when Scottie is silently stalking Madeleine, or searching for her in his misery after she has seemingly died. These passages in the music are dramatic interludes, as in an opera, that further the action while also commenting upon it. *Pygmalion* is not operatic at all, and despite its excellence as a musical, neither is *My Fair Lady*.

Shaw's version of the Pygmalion myth also overlaps with the Cinderella tale. His having recognized their connection is evident in the explanation he gives for calling the play a romance:

"It is a story of a poor girl who meets a gentleman at a church door, and is transformed by him, like Cinderella, into a beautiful lady. That is what I call a romance."[12]

The magicality of filmmaking lends itself to the Cinderella legend better than any literary work can, and in ways that run parallel to the pervasive artificiality of operatic music. Like the cinematography of *Pygmalion*, a Cinderella film can show us—in a flash of sparkling lights—the coach as it is instantaneously manufactured out of a pumpkin (together, perhaps, with the mice, the lizards, and the fat rat that become attendants and the coachman mentioned by Charles Perrault in his telling of the story at the end of the seventeenth century). In their partial reliance upon factuality, the play and the film *Pygmalion* employ a modification of that effect. At the end of the first act, Eliza enters a London taxi as if it were the coach that will lead her to her great adventure. It is only a quasi-magical conveyance, but it takes her to the superior dimensions of society for which she hungers. Since films can show more than is evident on stage, we observe the vehicle in motion as it wends its way to Eliza's dismal room, from which she will now make her escape.

The money that Eliza uses for the taxi is given to her by Higgins after he hears the chiming of bells outside the church in Covent Garden. Honegger's music enlarges their relevance by insinuating angelic chords of female voices, which Higgins takes as "a reminder." We can interpret their celestial sounds as the divine origin of his superhuman mission to help sustain Eliza's self-improvement. As such, they befit the earliest version of the myth while also indicating the inaccuracy in Higgins's later claim, in one place, to have acted only as a professional instructor, and, in another, to have done what he did because of the fun of it. Like the original Pygmalion, he too has divine powers favored by the gods. The birds that flutter from their perch within the portico when the bells begin to chime are—as in Giotto—the bearers of his sacred destiny, as well as Eliza's. The descent of birds at that moment alerts us to the realization that what we are watching is not just a prosaic story, but rather a myth about the human soul.

In most tellings of the Cinderella tale, the task of astounding transformation is entrusted to a kindly maternal figure, as contrasted with the girl's actual parent in the world. The latter is often a horrid stepmother who has somehow trapped Cinderella's father and is unlovable in herself. The stepmother is therefore a variant of the witch or old hag in fables like the one about Hansel and Gretel. Destroying her is an act that liberates all the other children who have been cruelly objectified, reduced to gingerbread cookies or whatever. In avoiding the violence of this denouement by focusing on the benevolent wisdom that causes a Prince Charming to fall in love with a lowly though virtuous female, the Cinderella myth is indeed a romance. The Shavian derivation differs from all the others by introducing hardheaded questions about the personality of the two principals and why they might not want to team up in a marriage.

All the same, Shaw retains reminders of the Cinderella story by including cognates of the fairy godmother. In being the firm but well-intentioned housekeeper who bathes Eliza and sensibly stands between her and Higgins from the very beginning, Mrs. Pearce is a resourceful and kindly mother type. Though the exceptional but ignorant girl grumbles about some of her restrictions, Eliza knows that Mrs. Pearce has a heart that is in the right place. At a higher level, Higgins's mother is also a protector of Eliza. In the last act, she even treats her like a favored daughter in her house. Yet neither of these older women serves as a wonder-worker, since that role is reserved for the magisterial Higgins. As a richer and better educated associate of Alfred Doolittle, he is equivalent to the magical godfather who stages Cinderella's transformation in some versions of that myth. In Rossini's opera *La Cenerentola,* for instance, there are two ugly sisters who maltreat the young girl but no mother or godmother. Instead Cinderella's apotheosis is produced by a godfather who, like God the Father, sees into her soul and enables her to be rewarded for her goodness. In Sturges's *The Palm Beach Story,* the "weenie king" whose fanciful gift launches the dissatisfied wife on her great exploits performs a similar function.

While he assists in abetting this kind of occurrence, Higgins is himself a wunderkind who is frequently reprimanded for his childishness and social ineptitude by Mrs. Pearce as well as by his mother. In his impish way, Shaw wrings this disparity for all its comical worth—the man of remarkable intellect shown to be incapable of the trivialities of social behavior that most lesser human beings carry out habitually and without excessive strain. Compared to her more worldly sisters, Cinderella generally has the simplicity of a child. In the alembic of Shaw's imagination, this link to divine innocence is present also in the childishness of Higgins. It makes him as lovable as our image of Albert Einstein in his old age. Einstein became a mythic hero for many people because he was a genius who stuck out his tongue in photographs and appeared in public wearing sneakers but no socks. Ovid would have relished that metamorphosis.[13]

3

The Heiress and *Washington Square*

It is often said that great works of literature do not lend themselves to the making of great films, either because the art modalities are too different or because the subtlety and inventiveness of the former are inevitably diminished by the visual contrivances in the latter. As a corollary, we are told, films are invariably, or generally, inferior to the novels from which they are derived. In *Reality Transformed: Film as Meaning and Technique*, I argued extensively that a sharp demarcation between the literary and the visual leads to basic misconceptions about the nature of film. The other dogma, about movies being inherently worse than their originating literary sources, seems to me equally questionable. In this regard the relationship between Henry James's novel *Washington Square* and the two outstanding films that have issued from it is especially interesting for several reasons. One of those movies, William Wyler's *The Heiress* (1949), is a masterpiece; and the other, Agnieszka Holland's *Washington Square* (1997) is quite good as well. Both films draw upon mythological motifs and have philosophical scope of their own. Each of them gives us ample material for reopening the aesthetic issues implied by the dubious assumptions I have just mentioned.

The novel by James was written within a year of the publication of his book on Hawthorne in which he indicates his desire to get beyond the literature of romance and into the kind of storytelling that directly portrays everyday reality. For such realism, which James maintains throughout the structure of *Washington Square,* he would scarcely wish to present anything that might be considered explicit mythology. And yet, the imagination of an author often defeats his or her intentions. As I will try to show, the Jamesian novel is best understood in relation to major myths of love that have developed over centuries in Western culture. That alone may constitute the bond between the mentality of James and the movies that his fiction spawned.

The relevant myths are not purely literary. They occur in opera, spoken drama for the stage, film, and all other visual production that has representational content. Collateral as they often are, works in these different arts need not be adaptations of each other. Though the sharing of affective mythology can provide a stereoscopic effect, an aesthetic object attains an indigenous quality by employing techniques that define its medium as well as the meanings proffered by some artist who generates its creative elements. And since artists are free to use the technical devices of their medium as they wish, so too do they reconstitute the inherited myths in accordance with their personal view of human nature.

Treating James's *Washington Square* as a case history, I discuss what I consider to be five transformational entities. They are as follows: the original story James heard from his friend Fanny Kemble; the novel James subsequently wrote; the play *The Heiress* that Ruth and Augustus Goetz fashioned based on the novel; the Wyler film that contains a scenario written by the Goetzes as an adaptation of their play; and the more recent film version of the novel that was directed by Holland. Within this gamut, there are significant differences among the mythological conceptions as well as the techniques of the various media. By studying these differences, we may also discern how their mythic components interact.

To show the emanation of the cinematic productions from their literary source, and their joint reliance upon themes that are common to them all, we might profitably start with analyses of the two movies. That is how film scholars have typically presented their material. In the case of James's *Washington Square*, however, I feel that it warrants extensive study in advance on its own and as a preparation for understanding the aesthetics of its transformation into the movies and the play that are autonomous though not wholly independent works of art.

I begin with the anecdote because it obviously came first. But that too is a kind of fable, a myth about the nature of the creative mind. It invokes a picture of an artist, an author in this circumstance, having a chat with a friend who mentions in a socially communicative exchange a situation in which her brother was involved. This information enters the presumably receptive but unformed mind of the artist, where it is altered by some chemistry of his or her imagination and finally issues into words that are written on the page. But we may well wonder whether creativity operates in so simplistic a manner. Is it not more likely that the Henry James who frequented such occasions was the embodiment of a mind that actively sought out the events, the relations, the recounted anecdotal evidence that it could use to investigate aspects of life that were already meaningful to its probing orientation?

I am not suggesting that James himself was aware of this propensity on his part. As he dressed to go to the tea or dinner party at which he would meet Mrs. Kemble, he may have expected and desired little more than an agreeable gathering at which there would be casual conversation, good food, handsome and well-dressed people to observe, and possibly a new acquaintance to be made. He might have had no idea that his artistic soul was searching for the nourishment it required in its continuous effort to make sense of the world inhabited by its native organism. Yet that would be a substantial part of what was going on.

Only rarely does an artist behave like Bloch, the character in Proust whose appearance in high society surprises the narrator. When asked why he is there, in view of his unfavorable attitude toward the rich and famous, Bloch replies: "J'observe." There is, of course, a menacing tone in that response, as if Bloch intends to get proof of the worthlessness of these people. But Proust interprets the anomaly of Bloch's occurrence in this elite company as an indication of his hypocrisy and self-deceit. His pretense of aesthetic and moral detachment is just a mask for the social climbing that really motivates him.

More representative of the creative artist is the presentation of Mozart in Miklos Forman's film *Amadeus*. After Mozart and his nascent family are having financial difficulties, we see his mother-in-law berate him as a ne'er-do-well who has betrayed his promise to take good care of her daughter. The voice of the incensed woman rises and falls in a passionate display of outraged fury. Mozart stares at her and listens without replying.

Having watched scenes in which the mother had schemed to capture the composer as a splendid marital acquisition, we identify with him. In our absorption in his life story, we experience the event from the perspective of a genius who suffers unfairly in his marriage. But, as we immediately learn, that is only a minor element in this scene. Without any intrusive commentary, it dissolves into the musical construction that fills Mozart's mind as he listens to his wife's abusive mother and that now turns into the vindictive coloratura of the Queen of the Night's first aria in *The Magic Flute*. We are surprised, but delighted: so *that's* what was going on as Mozart silently submitted to his mother-in-law's tirade! Our psychologizing about marital problems may not have been irrelevant—indeed, it was even essential for appreciating the musical meaning of the aria—but a Mozart transcends such issues by reformulating them into raw material for what he produces as an artist.

For this reason, we may approach Fanny Kemble's account of her brother's abortive courting as itself a fictive and largely mythic statement. She was a successful actress, and we can assume that her telling the anecdote was not unrelated to her personal creativity as a performer in the theater. Life is a walking shadow for everyone because we all strut and address one another like actors on a stage. In articulating this truth, Macbeth fails to remark that stage actors are also walking shadows, since their profession consists in projecting some imagined condition of ordinary humanity. In itself, that is performatory and inherently aesthetic through and through, whatever its degree of excellence as art may be. Moreover, the report that James presents is only his rendition of Mrs. Kemble's rendition. He writes it with the same mindset that pervades the novel he then derived from it, or rather extended beyond its limitations.

The novel is not identical with either Mrs. Kemble's narration or James's account of it. Yet all three are imbued with mythic motifs that recur and force us to perceive them as mutually overlapping.

Though James's paragraph will be familiar to some readers, it is worth repeating here. In his notebooks, an entry dated February 21, 1879, reads as follows:

Mrs. Kemble told me last evening the history of her brother H.'s engagement to Miss T. H. K. was a young ensign in a marching regiment, very handsome ("beautiful") said Mrs. K., but very luxurious and selfish, and without a penny to his name. Miss T. was a dull, plain, commonplace girl, only daughter of the Master of King's Coll., Cambridge, who had a very handsome private fortune (£4,000 a year). She was very much in love with K., and was of that slow, sober, nature that an impression once made upon her, was made forever. Her father disapproved strongly (and justly) of the engagement and informed her that if she married young K. he would not leave her a penny of his money. It was only in her money that H. was interested; he wanted a rich wife who would enable him to live at his ease and pursue his pleasures. Miss T. was in much tribulation and she asked Mrs. K. what she would advise her to do—Henry K. having taken the ground that if she would hold on and marry him the old Doctor would after a while relent and they should get the money. (It was in this belief that he was holding on to her.) Mrs. K. advised the young girl by *no means* to marry her brother. "If your father does relent and you are well off, he will make you a kindly enough husband, so long as all goes well. But if he should not, and you were to be poor, your lot would be miserable. *Then* my brother would be a very uncomfortable companion—*then* he would visit upon you his disappointment and discontent." Miss T. reflected a while; and then, as she was much in love with [him], she determined to disobey her father and take the consequences. Meanwhile H. K., however, had come to the conclusion that the father's forgiveness was not to be counted upon—that his attitude was very firm and that if they should marry he would never see the money. *Then* all his effort was to disentangle himself. He went off, shook himself free of the engagement, let the girl go. She was deeply wounded—they separated. Some years elapsed—her father died and she came into his fortune. She never received the addresses of another man—she always cared in secret for Henry K.—but she was determined to remain unmarried. K. lived about the world in different military stations, and at last, at the end of 10 years (or more), came back to England—still a handsome, selfish, impecunious soldier. One of his other sisters (Mrs. S.) then attempted to bring on the engagement again—knowing that Miss T. still cared for him. She tried to make Mrs. K. join her in this undertaking, but the latter refused, saying that it was speculation and that her brother had forfeited every claim to be being thought well of by Miss T. But K. again, on his own responsibility, paid his addresses to Miss T. She refused him—it was too late. And yet, said Mrs. K., she cared for him—and she would have married no other man. But H. K.'s selfishness had over-reached itself and this was the retribution of time.[1]

The retribution of time? Yet our summary conceptions of human response include other explanatory tropes. We say that time heals all, that in time a man or woman comes to wisdom, that temporal as well as spatial distance makes the heart grow fonder. Though H. K.'s character had not altered, Miss T. might well have thrown herself into his arms as the intended culmination of her earlier attachment. She could have done so in the enactment of a lingering passion that lay dormant throughout the intervening years, or else in recognition of the fact that H. was the only man she had ever really "cared for." She might have deluded herself about the extent of his selfishness or else, with the insight and depth of feeling that time sometimes brings, she could have found within herself a compassionate urge to cure him of his moral disabilities. As James presents the facts conveyed to him by Mrs. Kemble, these possibilities do not apply. She does not ascribe the outcome to "the retribution of time." James says this, at the end of his account, in a statement that voices his own view of Miss T.'s decision. It is the only perspective he seems willing to entertain.

With that as the basis of his retention of what Mrs. Kemble may have said, James is intrigued by the paradoxical nature of Miss T.'s attitude. "And yet, said Mrs. K., she cared for him—and she would have married no other man." We must imagine James asking himself how and why this can be. If, for whatever reason and regardless of the time that has elapsed, someone cares for another person as Miss T. still does (we are not told that she cares less for Henry now than she did before), is it not likely that the individual will seek the same consummation as was previously desired? Human nature being what it is, this is a reasonable supposition, a plausible conception of what Miss T. would do. We know that people are often fickle in their emotions, and that a jilted woman might never forgive the man who caused her such deep-rooted pain. But the fact that Miss T. *still cares* for Henry would seem to override that pattern of response. In a common strain of nineteenth-century romanticism, love forever craves completion and, if it perdures as Miss T.'s has, it seeks the same or similar oneness—marriage, in her case—that was desperately wanted at an earlier time.

James focuses on the paradoxical avoidance of this conclusion because he wishes to move beyond the Romantic mythology he has repudiated. He employs the historical actuality as a real and unmistakable phenomenon in the lives of men and women, albeit one that stands in need of a more accurate and graphic portrayal of human feeling. The anecdote he hears and molds to his own authorial bent is valuable to him because it delineates in narrative form a large-scale problem that requires analysis and resolution.

The details of the situation are not themselves at all exceptional. Young girls have always fallen in love with dashing soldiers and very handsome men, above all when they are soldiers who are *both* dashing and very handsome. Repressive fathers have regularly tried to control the amatory experience of their young daughters. The fathers have in hand the family money, and they know that by withholding it in the present and in the future they can have the greatest effect upon their daughters' choice of a husband. Sometimes, as in *King Lear*, the fathers use their monetary power to secure for themselves the love of their daughters. But more often, they prefer to buy a son-in-law who are acceptable in their judgment regardless of what their female children may prefer. That is the premise of *A Midsummer Night's Dream*, and of countless other courtship tales. It had been a stock-in-trade of romanesque novels ever since the Hellenistic period. The young people have to find a way to circumvent parental repressiveness, and in the fables their efforts frequently succeed. Moreover, they are presumed to live happily ever after. In Mrs. Kemble's anecdote that assurance underlies Miss T.'s decision to defy her father whether or not he finally relents and lets her have the money anyhow. In considering this phenomenon in his revisionist way, James voices the viewpoint of a counterculture that arose in the latter half of the nineteenth century and has continued up to the present.

In Western love literature the male suitor has often been presented as selfish and aggressive, prone to treat women as commodities, whether sexually or monetarily. What James must have found perplexing was the possibility that Miss T.

loved Henry even though she realized he was that kind of man. Despite her rejection of Mrs. Kemble's advice, she is not reported as having doubted her diagnosis of her brother's character. Was Miss T. courting danger because love had suborned her rationality, or was she impelled by greater and deeper motives? The traditional myths of love do not investigate this kind of question at any length. From his vantage point in history, James saw that as an opportunity for himself.

The matter becomes a recurrent theme in James's writing. Throughout his middle period, to which *Washington Square* belongs, and into his final works, he is fascinated by the spectacle of women in love with men who either misuse them or are morally deficient in their relations with them. Whether the men are cold and calculating, like Osmond in *The Portrait of a Lady*, or themselves ensnared and corrupted by love, like Densher in *The Wings of the Dove*, or gentle but weak fortune hunters, like Amerigo in *The Golden Bowl*, they prey upon women who must ultimately accommodate their own loving attitude to the moral inferiority of the male. These works generate a conundrum, and an aura of mythological fable, out of the problematics in that situation. If we choose, we can see them all as stemming from Mrs. Kemble's anecdote, though being differently inspired by it. At the same time I think it is plausible to say that James had been intrigued by her account because of forces—hidden from our view perhaps—that caused this kind of human experience to be deeply meaningful for him.

What James addresses, embellishes but also scrutinizes throughout his fiction, is largely insoluble, not only because of its infinite diversity in relations between men and women but also because it can have no definitive resolution. The most a creative writer can do with it is to present the configuration of a representative example, to help us imagine people being beset by it within the parameters of one or another social setting, to depict the feelings that make the condition so compelling in a person's life, and so difficult to overcome with any degree of equanimity or satisfaction. There is no right or wrong ending to be found—human beings are too complex for that, and the great variety in possible behavior rules out any likelihood of recognized certitude. Yet we in the audience are able to sense that we have grappled with something that is profoundly important in our common reality. Therein lies the mythic profundity.

If the mythmaker is a storyteller who offers us a written narrative encasing the rudimentary facts, we call him or her a novelist. But this does not prevent us from viewing the enterprise as philosophical. An explicit moralist who does not need any elaborate tale of fiction we might be willing to call a philosopher. The moralist and the novelist are equally philosophical, however, inasmuch as they are alike in their reliance upon a broad and gripping system of issues that cannot be classified as scientific or merely empirical. When a perceptive presentation of the problems is combined with an effort to analyze their multiple implications, what results is a work of what may be called either philosophical literature or literary philosophy. Without having necessarily reasoned it through, that is what directed James's imagination as he listened to Mrs. Kemble and progressively gleaned the mythic sediment in what she said.

James begins his novel as if it were just a memoir or biography of actual persons in American history: "During a portion of the first half of the present century, and more particularly during the latter part of it, there flourished and practiced in the city of New York a physician who enjoyed perhaps an exceptional share of the consideration which, in the United States, has always been bestowed upon distinguished members of the medical profession."[2] Writing in 1880 under the influence of realists like Ivan Turgenev and Guy de Maupassant, James was immediately, from the very outset, informing his readers that he would not be telling a romanesque story of the sort that Nathaniel Hawthorne might have written. It was to be a tale that had sociological significance and quasi-scientific precision. Note his qualification about the temporal demarcation: not just a portion of the first half of the century but "more particularly" the latter part of the first half. The remainder of that paragraph then expatiates upon the esteem that Americans have always accorded members of the medical profession. We are even given an explanation of why this is so.

But once we have finished the novel, and to some extent as we are going through it, we realize that this preparatory note has a function far beyond its sociological import. It is a key or clue that admits us to the world of myth and fable that James has distilled out of the temporal events he claims to be elucidating. Why are American doctors, specifically those who live in New York in the middle of the nineteenth century, held in such high honor? Because their profession belongs to the realm of the practical and is associated with the scientific, both of these being exceptional values "in a country in which, to play a social part, you must either earn your income or make believe that you earn it."[3] In asserting the truth of this, the generalization enunciates a network of ideals that in their entirety represent the mythological basis for what the novel then depicts. This myth about what is and what is not acceptable in that specified society serves as a silver nail, as James might call it, that fastens our aesthetic involvement to the fictional narrative he presents.

Boiled down to its simplest outline, the fable recounts a continuing duel between two men, one of whom earns his income and enjoys a position in New York society as a respectable physician, the other of whom claims that he will shortly earn whatever money he requires in order to live comfortably as a member of that society. As a matter of fact, he sponges on his sister during most of the novel and never does succeed in any gainful employment. The principal males thereby reenact the struggle between the Master of King's College, Cambridge, and the hapless soldier who tries to outmaneuver him.

Transferred to the American scene, the younger man does not have a social role as someone who makes a living by killing enemies of his country, but like his English counterpart he, too, is dashing and very handsome. The two relationships between father and suitor are similar in being generational, an older versus a younger man, and they both center around the sexual and marital state of a young woman whom one of them possesses as an only daughter and the other wants to acquire as a wealthy wife. In the history of affective imagination in the West, this recapitulates the fundamental structure of the Don Juan myth. James's opening paragraph introduces that motif as emphatically as the first scene in Mozart's *Don Giovanni*. Mozart immediately proceeds to show us the two men in a literal duel, but James is more deliberative and feels the need for lengthier exposition. Retaining his veneer as a realistic storyteller, he tries to explain how this male conflict can occur within the framework of its historical situation. That attempt underlies his minute exposition—much more thorough than anything an opera can present—of the ramifications within that conflict.

Between Tirso de Molina's play about an erotic trickster of Seville and James's novel about the deceptiveness of a con man who resembles him, more than two hundred years elapsed. Though social customs had altered in both Europe and America, the nature of intrafamily power had scarcely changed. Not all young women in New York around 1850 were as dependent on their fathers as Catherine was, but their submission to his command remained the governing principle. Though the nineteenth-century equivalents of Doña Ana had more freedom to circumvent the authority of the patriarch, their equilibrations occurred within constraints that were very much like those imposed on the Spanish predecessor. In Tirso de Molina, or even Mozart, we get only glimmers of the independent spirit that causes Catherine to react to her predicament as she does. In James, and in the cinematic adaptations of his novel, her strength of purpose becomes a motor that propels the plot. Far from lessening the relevance of the Don Juan myth, her determination enlivens it and gives it a role in the modern world.

In the earlier versions of the myth, the autocratic father figure, ossified as a person before Don Juan kills him and he becomes a statue, wreaks revenge upon the young seducer by dragging him down to hell. Ana plays no part in this event. It is a matter between men, something to be settled by them in accordance with their usual ideas about honor, virility, and the aggressive violence that justifies itself as moral rectitude. In James the woman at stake begins as a passive daughter who then awakens to her own autonomy merely by falling and remaining in love with a man her father does not deem eligible. In Tirso de Molina, too, the problems of Ana originate with her secretly meeting Don Ottavio, whom she loves and who would doubtless have been acceptable to her father as a husband but not as a clandestine visitor to her bedchamber. Masquerading as Don Ottavio, Don Juan may well have felt justified in poaching a female who has made herself accessible in this illicit manner. She has evaded the sexual mores that men have unilaterally established. Neither in Tirso de Molina nor in most of the later variants of the Don Juan myth does the Ana character develop to a point where she is able to absolve herself or bring her apparent waywardness to its final justification.

The Catherine that James creates is entirely different. Not only does she enter into a courtship that her father has not sanctioned, but also she tells him of her engagement before her suitor has officially asked for her hand in marriage. The normal procedure—normal at that time—ratifies the father's position as the head of the family who has a right to decide as he wishes about a daughter's marital preference. Having taken the initiative on her own, which actually impairs her chances of persuading her father, Catherine then joins forces with her lover and her aunt in jockeying to get the old man to agree. At the end it is she who vengefully punishes the Don Juan surrogate she had wanted to marry. Having been jilted, she casts him off although she still cares for him. Surviving, in the manner that she does, she *becomes* her father. She has achieved a position of respect and social standing comparable to what his had been; she lives, by herself except for Aunt Lavinia, in the beautiful house where once he ruled; she ends up being virtually the sole remaining member of the doomed family that will now end with her. Unlike Ana or her earlier forebears in the myth, Catherine terminates her father's genetic line. That biological failure is both her liberation and her retribution upon him.

Apart from peripheral personages like Mrs. Almond, Dr. Sloper's sensible sister, and Mrs. Montgomery, who is

Morris Townsend's sister, the novel concentrates upon the four principal characters. Two are men: Sloper and Morris; two are women: Lavinia and Catherine. The men compete with each other, but so do the women. In both cases, it is a struggle between an older man or woman and a young man or woman. The older man dominates the older woman, and at first the young man dominates the young woman. But she is the final victor in this rectangular struggle. Though badly bruised, she emerges as the only person who benefits from their mutual agony. She alone achieves the kind of self-awareness that James valued above all other human attainments.

In her study of the novel, Millicent Bell touches on the concepts of cleverness and naturalness that collide within it. She rightly points out the father's consecration to cleverness and Lavinia's repeated deviations from it. But except for the moment in the Alps when Sloper admits he is a passionate man, willful in his craving for control, Bell claims that only Catherine can be thought truly "natural."[4] Yet Morris speaks of himself that way. Bell dismisses his assertion as the guilefulness of a cunning seducer. She may be right, but the matter needs further study: it is central to our understanding of what the novel is all about.

Such queries are normally, and sometimes reliably, resolved by asking what the author had in mind, as indicated either by the intentions he manifests within the novel or by those to which he testifies once he has finished it. With that as the criterion, we may well conclude that Morris is interested only in the girl's money. Mrs. Kemble's anecdote that James reports in explaining how the novel got written in the first place is predicated upon this assumption. Even so, works of art, like human beings, often evolve into something very different from what anyone—including their creator—might have foreseen. And once the product has been completed, even the creator may not truly recognize what he has done. The Old Testament is proof of that.

In whatever medium, works of art are like human beings, or societies, or other groups of individuals, that attain their own reality through some process of inner development. The artist, or whoever makes the artwork, may not be wholly conscious of what the creative activity was bringing into being. This kind of uncertainty preoccupied James in everything he wrote. It reaches an aesthetic peak in *The Turn of the Screw*, a tale within a tale, the overt story being a reenactment of what the governess has imparted to the narrator. Her personal role in the narrative permeates everything she describes, but James gives us no way of determining whether she is telling the truth or merely revealing her own delusions. Far from offering evidence that would enable us to reach a conclusive judgment, James emphasizes the ambiguity and indecipherability of all the information that he dispassionately presents. What starts out as a possible ghost story changes into a study of inductive, and other, means by which human beings seek knowledge or merely clarification about the contents of their own experience.

Washington Square is less ambitious in this regard than *The Turn of the Screw*. It is less concerned about raising epistemological problems in what purports to be a realistic portrayal. While *The Turn of the Screw* appears to be more factual insofar as the governess's story is the testament of someone who claims to have lived through the actual occurrences, unverifiable as this may be, *Washington Square* emanates from the pen of a detached though seemingly omniscient author whose verisimilitude style of writing delineates what happened at a particular time in a place we know and to people who could certainly have been there then. All the same, James sprinkles the latter narration with bits of contrary evidence that undermines, to some degree, his more or less explicit hints about the characters' motivation.

For instance, having led us to believe that Morris is a gigolo, and as selfish as Mrs. Kemble's brother, James modifies his portrait in ways that give it more depth but also make us wonder what Morris is really like. As a work of art, the novel is superior, far superior, to Mrs. Kemble's remarks precisely because of the enrichment James introduces by means of ambiguities such as this one. Dr. Sloper concludes that Morris is a fortune hunter and insists that nineteen times out of twenty his diagnoses are correct. But we know that not even a reliable statement of probabilities can be a priori certain, and also that the remaining instance, the twentieth diagnosis, may always vitiate the doctor's assertion. Love trades upon the uniqueness of each person, bestowing value upon the individuality of his or her being. What Sloper says seems justifiable in terms of statistics, but it cannot encompass the specific attachment that love itself creates. Through this chink in the armor of mere rationality, the glimmer of uncertainty enters and establishes itself as a disturbing factor in our beliefs about the relationship between Catherine and Morris.

Having read the witty and sometimes derogatory remarks that Morris launches freely at Lavinia, his foolish but well-intentioned ally in the battle against Sloper, we may feel encouraged to think that the doctor is right in denying that the supercilious Morris can truly love Catherine. And yet James also gives the suitor words that make us reconsider. In his studied openness and constant perspicacity, Morris tells Catherine at the start that her father does not like him. When she asks how he can know that, he replies: "I feel; I am very quick to feel."[5] Is this just the manner of a sly predator who must have rapid and accurate intuitions in order to elude detection? Or is it a sign of emotional sensitivity in a vulnerable and mainly innocent lover like those that the Romantics idealized throughout the nineteenth century?

That the Morris whom James has created belongs to that genre more than James may himself have realized is suggested by something else that pertains to this novel. I have in mind his extreme reluctance, here as throughout his other fiction, to give us intimate, particularly sexual, details of people bonding with each other during their moments of privacy. His books are often organized as vehicles designed to show how hard it is to know what really happens when people are venting their strongest feelings. At the same time, he recognizes the importance of those feelings and vividly signals their occurrence with red or black flags that tell us how turbulent and dangerous the tide may be at this point. But as in the case of the ocean markings on the beach, it is one thing to learn what must be going on and another to observe directly, though in imagination, some instance of erotic upheaval. Inferential procedures may provide knowledge of sexual experience, and even yield the great excitement of progressively amassing such knowledge, but that alone cannot provide a simulacrum of the actual quality of those feelings.

James tells us that Morris and Catherine have sessions of intimacy, yet their components are rarely portrayed. They are generally adduced from Catherine's point of view, and so we might well think that her spontaneous joy in them is to be taken as only a sign of girlish infatuation. For all we know, she may be wholly deluded by the love she has fallen into.

Since James wants to chart Catherine's cognitive as well as affective growth throughout a long-term period of self-realization, he carefully demarcates the stages of her emotional and intellectual awakening. That is what creates her ability to forge her own destiny instead of remaining a pawn of male predilections. It also means, however, that we must give *some* credence to her judgment about Morris's motivation, and whether his feelings toward her are real rather than springes to catch a wealthy woodcock. In the novel, though not in Mrs. Kemble's statement, the question remains: How much credence can be justified in this regard?

Since James is so loathe to state what happens when lovers are alone with each other, and since we are rarely given admittance into Morris's consciousness as he himself experiences it, we have to gather our data from the scenes in which he charms Catherine or spars with Sloper as his male opponent. The most confrontational of these occurs after Catherine has informed her father that she plans to marry Morris. But prior to that, there is the tête-à-tête in which Morris proposes marriage to her and she agrees.

The earlier chapter ends with Morris kissing Catherine and James commenting coyly: "This is all that need be recorded of their conversation."[6] Agreement having been reached by the man and woman, we are left to surmise the words of endearment they will now express to each other. Yet the chapter begins in a fashion that disposes us to question Morris's sincerity. It shows him coolly calculating his next move as he waits for

Catherine in the parlor of her fine house. Talking to himself, he says: "'We must settle something—we must take a line,' he declared, passing his hand through his hair and giving a glance at the long, narrow mirror which adorned the space between the two windows, and which had at its base a little gilded bracket covered by a thin slab of white marble, supporting in its turn a backgammon board folded together in the shape of two volumes—two shining folios inscribed, in greenish-gilt letters, *History of England*."[7]

The realistic depiction of this suitor calmly assuring himself about his appearance in a mirror whose embellishments bespeak the pretentiousness of mid-Victorian claims to respectable culture suggests that while Morris's inclinations at the moment may be amatory they are probably not heartfelt. We next see him maneuver Catherine through crucial preliminaries to their engagement. Having stated that he adores her, he gets her to agree that they must "settle" things right away. This means informing her father, which Morris would be expected to do. But then he makes a tactical blunder. He yields to Catherine's desire that she tell her father of their wishes before Morris formally requests her hand in marriage. Acceding to that plan of action, Morris carefully tells Catherine how to parry what he knows will be her father's insistence that this suitor's interests are wholly mercenary. He does not foresee that Sloper will interpret her being the initiator as further proof of Morris's unprincipled scheming.

In his conversations with Catherine and with Morris in subsequent chapters, the father takes umbrage at the fact that Morris has not come to him directly. Dueling with Morris at this juncture, the father makes this his first thrust. It scores a point for him because it proves that Morris does not adhere to the unspoken codes of propriety. Though he comes from a good family—albeit on its peripheries—and though he is eloquent, handsome, well-dressed, and with tastes like the father's, he falls short as a prospective son-in-law. In the verbal swordplay that ensues, he stands up well nevertheless. He bravely forces the doctor to confess that his negative attitude is based on knowledge of Morris's poverty and belief that Catherine is "a weak young woman with a large fortune." Morris denies, correctly as we later learn, that Catherine is weak; and he pushes Sloper into admitting that his resistance does reflect his awareness of Morris's financial condition. "Even if she were not weak," the father says, "you would still be a penniless man." To this, Morris answers: "Ah, yes, that is *my* weakness! And therefore, you mean, I am mercenary—I only want your daughter's money."

Sloper replies: "I don't say that. . . . I say simply that you belong to the wrong category." Morris ably fends this off in a manner that appeals to the reader's romantic and egalitarian sentiments: "'But your daughter doesn't marry a category,' Townsend urged, with his handsome smile. 'She marries an individual—an individual whom she is so good as to say she loves.'" And as against the charge that he is "an individual who offers so little in return," he securely asks: "Is it possible to offer more than the most tender affection and a lifelong devotion?"[8]

When the debate continues along these lines, Morris insists that his affection for Catherine is "as pure and disinterested a sentiment as was ever lodged in a human breast. I care no more for her fortune than for the ashes in that grate."[9] The climax of the story proves this to be false. But the reader has no way of knowing that in advance. Despite the distrust of Morris's motivation that has been awakened in us, his responses to

Sloper's rejection of him are fairly persuasive. How else could a man in love be expected to profess the purity of his feelings? It is Sloper, if anyone, who seems to have a mercenary outlook. His saying that Catherine is weak and without charm, neither of which is the case, makes us suspicious of the authenticity of his constant emphasis upon her money.

And yet, despite pervasive squabbling over the disposition of Catherine's inheritance, money is not the principal theme in this novel. Though James never lets us forget that Morris, Catherine, and Sloper belong to an upper-middle-class society in which the accumulation and display of wealth are prerequisites for respectability, he never shows us people in the process of acquiring money or spending it or using it in any significant way that is beneficial to them. The husband of Catherine's cousin Marian is a stockbroker who knows the social and economic value of moving uptown as the city grows northward, but there is no suggestion of a monetary basis to that marital union. Similarly, Catherine and her fanciful aunt Lavinia take it for granted that money is a good thing to possess throughout one's married life, but for them it is something they have effortlessly enjoyed since childhood.

For his part, Morris—who has squandered his own inheritance and now lives "on the remnants of [his] property"—knows that the sweetness and the elegance of a cultivated life necessitates the kind of leisure that costs a lot of money. Once he has been rejected by Sloper and treated as an outsider who wants to steal the family jewels, he raises the price on himself, so to speak. Only after he feels the insult in Sloper's treatment of him does he fight to acquire Catherine's twenty-thousand-dollar legacy as well as her own fortune of ten thousand dollars. The struggle with the father seems to have made the difference.

For Sloper the situation is comparable in reverse. However much he talks about the money, there is something else at stake for him as well. The twenty thousand are his as long as he lives, and he knows that even if he gives them to charity instead of to Catherine, her ten thousand plus ownership of the mansion in Washington Square is more than enough to assure a very pleasant life in good society. He tells Morris he fears that as her husband he will squander Catherine's wealth. Morris admits that in the instability of youth he did misuse his own money, but he insists that he is now wiser and less reckless. Sloper prefers to think that he is just selfish. Yet he has no grounds for this belief, apart from the subsequent testimony of Mrs. Montgomery, Morris's sister. I will return to her statements later on. They count heavily in the novel, as their equivalent does in Mrs. Kemble's report about herself and her brother. But in James the doctor seeks out the sister as one who can provide confirmation for what he has already concluded on the basis of very little evidence. What then is the source of Sloper's opposition, and how is it the counterpart of what Morris feels?

For both Morris and Sloper the prime factor in their argument is the characteristic male quest for power, and the vindication of one's intrinsic right to exercise it. For Sloper, the disposition of the family money is important because it is the symbol of his supremacy as the man who has augmented it through his legitimate labors. For Morris, the funds in question signify the valuable things of life that he feels he has earned simply by knowing how to enjoy them better than most people. The men are opposed to each other for reasons of pride and self-assertion, a mythic motif that has caused males to fight since the beginning of time. It alienates an older man from one who is young and vigorous and capable of savoring the benefits of wealth; and it alienates the younger man from a parental icon who thinks his experience and protective intentions entitle him to the privileges of absolute command and unquestionable authority.

The same holds for most of the other versions of the Don Juan myth, except that the explicit cause of conflict in them has usually been libidinal sex rather than money. Commentators who speak of the doctor acting as if his daughter were his legitimate and exclusive possession, as one's money is in a capitalist society, are right, but they usually fail to probe the meaning of possessiveness.[10] To possess something, above all if one has worked to get it, is to have a feeling of justifiable right to dispose of it as one wishes. To have mixed one's labor with material goods, as John Locke says of private property in general, is to have merged one's identity with the physical world in a way that gives a person special prerogative over it. It has become a part of oneself, like the food that is swallowed and then digested. That attitude, misguided as it may be, is what occasions Sloper's revulsion toward Morris as a son-in-law. Being outsiders to the narrative, we might reply that Morris does belong to an acceptable category for marriage since he has put so much labor into successfully captivating Catherine, even though he has not shown himself worthy of her affection by earning the money on his own. This mode of thought has no place in Sloper's outlook.

Morris sees Sloper as a man who is and has everything Morris wants. Sloper sees Morris as a formidable competitor for the status that he has had, in society and in the family, throughout his married life. He recognizes the danger in the intellectual and ingratiating virtues of Morris, which he himself praises and honestly admires. He knows that anyone who is that accomplished might use his youthful allure to subvert the older man's dominance over Catherine as well as Lavinia. He must attack Morris, as he does in the verbal duel, and having attacked him he must defend both his negative assessment and his vaunted reputation for expert diagnosis that enables him to make that assessment. Though his stated fear is that Morris will somehow abscond with Catherine's fortune, this reasoning is propelled by the sheer dynamics of the power struggle with a threatening interloper. The phenomenon is preeminent in the upper echelons of baboon society and common among human beings.

Seen in that light, the apparent coldness of Sloper's personality takes on an emotional dimension that James mentions only occasionally in his role as narrator. Time and again he portrays Sloper as a highly cultivated medical technician with acute rationality. Sloper is described not only as a clever man but also as one who sees the world as a cluster of mathematical problems that can be solved by someone who has a brain like his own. In the midst of his ongoing attempt to defeat Catherine's hopes of marriage, he begins to weary of the challenge, as if it posed difficulties in geometry that are too easy to be of further interest. James would have us think of him as a scientistic person who believes that all affective matters are manageable by cognitive procedures. Only once does he lose his cool and give vent to tempestuous forces in himself that he usually keeps hidden.

That occurs when Catherine and he take their walk in a desolate region of the Alps. Having gone ahead, perhaps to frighten Catherine with the possibility of being abandoned by him, as he later asserts that Morris would do if she married him, he returns and interrogates her about her present views. When she tells him that despite her lengthy absence she has not given up on Morris, Sloper discloses what is lurking in his soul: "I am not a very good man. Though I am very smooth externally, at bottom I am very passionate, and I assure you I can be very hard."[11] He then tells her he is angry and has been "raging inwardly for the last six months."[12]

Except for his saying he is not a good man, which she cannot understand at all, Catherine is not fazed by these self-revelations. She considers it natural that her father should have strenuous feelings of disappointment at her resistance. She does not recognize that his tyrannical desire to control her spousal choice manifests a willful quest for mastery, which prevents him from understanding that Morris might indeed be a suitable husband for her.

Having learned in the first pages of the novel about the early death of Sloper's wife and son, we have reason to question Sloper's ability to administer, and to diagnose correctly, even the medical hazards that people face. Lavinia taunts him with his past failures, implying that he might also be incapable of appreciating Morris as he should. But neither she nor Catherine can comprehend why Sloper comes down so strongly in his abomination of him as a son-in-law. To prove his impartiality, Sloper invites Mrs. Montgomery to talk with him about her brother. He thinks her deposition will be definitive.

In treating the accumulation of evidence as a fundamental theme in this novel, as it most emphatically is in other works of his, particularly *The Turn of the Screw*, James depicts minutely the doctor's meeting with Mrs. Montgomery. Morris has been living with her and presumably tutoring her children. Though Sloper is certain that the young man is a selfish scoundrel, he goes in search of undeniable proof of his intuitive judgment.

The interview with Mrs. Montgomery occurs in each of the versions of the Jamesian legend, but there is nothing comparable in the original anecdote. There Mrs. Kemble warns the infatuated Miss T. that H. K. would make her married life a misery if the couple ever had to depend on him for their subsistence. When another sister of his later tries to intervene on his behalf, Mrs. Kemble refuses a second time to further his cause. James digests all that and expands it in several ways. He invents a sister, Mrs. Almond, who is more than just peripheral and who makes sensible comments about the family problem; he transforms Mrs. Kemble's sister into Aunt Lavinia, who has a primary role throughout the plot; and he gives an exhaustive account of Sloper's conversation with Mrs. Montgomery, with whom Morris is living. In the novel she finally takes a stand similar to Mrs. Kemble's. Nevertheless, Mrs. Montgomery's testimony is distinctly different in each of the cinematic transformations as well as in the play.

At this point we may leap into the two films adapted from the Jamesian source. Although Wyler's movie *The Heiress* relies on the native realism of a period piece and begins with a card that reads "A hundred years ago," it eschews the sociological generalizations that James presents in his attempt to maintain the historical accuracy of his account. Wyler was following the script of his scenarists, the Goetzes, who were remaining faithful to their stage version of James's novel. In calling both film and play *The Heiress,* they shifted the imagination of any possible audience into a category quite unlike the one that James addressed. His title referred to a specific locale in New York, in fact one that he had known as a child, whereas theirs summons up feelings we may have about someone who possesses, or will possess, a large amount of money. The geographical reference is not especially dramatic, even if we have knowledge about its relevance to the novelist's upper-class childhood. Not only does the image of an heiress prepare us for a tale about a particular individual but also it adumbrates a drama about the interpersonal problems that may descend upon someone who fits that description. In the Goetzes' play, there is no narrator. All the comments that James makes have been stripped away—his godlike awareness of what is happening in the minds of his characters as well as his comments as an accommodating guide to the recent development of neighborhoods in nineteenth-century New York City.

While staying close to the play's approach, and retaining most of its language, Wyler also opens it up to the many details that would not be worth including on stage. I will be mentioning several, but as a quick illustration note the early scene in which Catherine's delicacy of soul is manifested by her turning away when the fishmonger chops off the head of the fish he is selling her. Soon afterward she proudly shows her father what their evening meal will include and he very gently criticizes her for not having had the fishmonger deliver what she has purchased to the house. This tells us a great deal about the two of them, but on the stage it would be out of place and unneeded for the drama.

In going beyond the play, the Wyler film begins with a series of images of stitched embroidery that is pertinent to the story. The handiwork is highly stylized in a way that dates what will appear on-screen to some period in the past when women at home might be engaged in practicing that kind of domestic art. It especially belongs to the narrative that we will see in two important scenes. After Catherine has been ditched by Morris and is forced to remain in her father's house even though she cannot bear to live with him any longer, he comes upon her while she is working at her craft. She focuses on it with fixed intensity as a pretense for not looking at him, even when he speaks to her. At the end of the movie, when Morris returns to beg her forgiveness, she is close to completing the pattern she has been sewing. As an expression of her desire to terminate her lingering fixation upon him, she snips the last stitch with her scissors and declares that she will never embroider anything else. It is a gesture that parallels the fishmonger's chopping off the head of the fish he sells Catharine at the beginning of the film. Being sensitive, she had then closed her eyes and shuddered at the sound of the axe against the block. Now, in her hardened maturity, she resolutely confronts what she must do.

We may take this as reminiscent of what Ate enacts at her loom in Greek mythology when she destroys the lives of human beings by cutting the thread that symbolizes their individual continuance in time. But we cannot foresee this at our first viewing of the embroidery images that the introductory credits roll over. The music by Aaron Copland that we hear is also preparatory to the dramatic structure of the movie, though as yet telling us little about it. Like an overture to an opera, it draws upon a melody that will recur throughout the film as a mythic filament of its own that interweaves with the events being shown. The music is based on a French folk song that contains the words "Plaisirs d'amour ne durent qu'un moment; chagrins d'amour durent toute la vie" (The pleasures of love last for only a moment; the sorrows of love last all your life).

In the first presentation of this motif, Copland's construction is lush and intriguing in its orchestral fullness. It returns within the story when Morris plays it on the piano for Catherine and then feebly intones the words in an English translation. In the novel we are told that Morris is a somewhat accomplished singer, and he even performs a couple of solos in public. In the Wyler movie, Morris seems quite untrained, except in his artful ability to use music to arouse the erotic attention of an inexperienced young woman like Catherine. The song is totally new to her, and he plays it because he thinks she might find its words suggestive. It is part of his male repertoire designed to encourage a female's attraction to himself and to some intimate relationship with him.

We might wonder how parading the lasting suffering of love could serve his purpose as a pursuer of this shy and diffident person. Is it because he knows that beneath her Calvinist, at least puritan, veneer she longs for libidinal delights that will test her resolve even if she suffers in the process? In any event, Morris's tactic works, and he very quickly establishes in Catherine a state of love that is for her an ecstatic pleasure. The romantic fervor of their relationship reaches its high point when the two embrace passionately in downpouring rain on the night she comes home after the year her father has forced her to travel with him through Europe. At that moment, the "plaisirs d'amour" refrain soars triumphantly to signify the eternity of emotional oneness that Catherine, at least, anticipates. Their embrace is itself a partial consummation of what the music had promised at the start. There it ended once the credits did. After the introductory card about the time period, the embroidery morphs into a shot of carriages passing along the street in front of the Sloper mansion in Washington Square. All the ensuing drama takes place at that location.

Later in the film, when Catherine scurries out of the house because she mistakenly thinks Morris has come to take her away, Copland inserts energetic but dissonant chords in contrast to the melodious harmonies of the French tune about the joy and sadness of love. In an interview years afterward he tells us that he had originally scored much milder music in this place. He had to remove it because during the movie's tryout, at its prerelease, people in the audience laughed inexplicably. Copland claims not to know why the dissonance worked so well and was just right for that scene. Whatever the reason may be, the caustic sounds emphatically convince us that Catherine's romance will not continue to be pleasurable.

The recent Holland film differs from Wyler's in many details, some of them resulting from the fact that it is an adaptation not of a stage play, but rather of the James novel itself. Like the novel, the Holland story begins with the birth of Catherine and the concomitant death of her mother. The presiding doctor, Catherine's father, cowers in a corner, crushed by the event. Grieving the loss of his wife, he shows relative unconcern about their offspring. Having omitted all this, Wyler and the Goetzes insert, at the dance many years later, Sloper's remark to his sister Mrs. Almond that disparagingly compares Catherine with her mother. When Mrs. Almond complains that he has intolerably idealized the poor dead woman, he replies: "You are not entitled to say that: only I know what I lost when she died, and what I got in her place." This horrifying statement, as if mother and child are not persons to be accepted in themselves, as separate individuals, but instead evaluated on a scale of his own choosing that treats them like measurable commodities, tells us at this point a great deal about Sloper's distorted mentality. Holland evokes a comparable insight in the audience, but she does so in a gradual and novelistic progression that is less dramatic than Wyler's.

This alternate orientation enables Holland to depict, quite vividly, events that are coherent with the Jamesian text but not actually present in it. As one can imagine, the novel contains nothing like the scene in which Catherine at about ten years of age urinates uncontrollably in public and wets her clothes while trying to sing a little song at her birthday party. Without duplicating any of the discursive talk that James uses to speak as narrator, Holland's camera establishes the spatial and historical setting of the story with a long and leisurely tracking shot from a low-lying crane sweeping across the densely vegetated park that borders the house in which the initial action occurs.

More than in either the novel or the Wyler version, the park itself then becomes the scene of later events. The film credits are superimposed on it. This bit of cinematography is excellent, but it does not convey the upper-middle-class sense of isolated exclusivity that one gets from Wyler's concentration upon the noble façade of the house and its position in the midst of tall, iron railings that protectively stand before it like all the other homes on this block. Holland's images of children playing in the park suggest a lively family neighborhood that neither James nor Wyler had in mind. A director is certainly free to make a decision such as Holland's, but one tends to regret that we are introduced to the narrative by neither a quasi-sociological frame as in James nor the more theatrically dramatic one that Wyler imposes from the start.

Among the most striking differences between the two movies is their divergent presentation of the scene between Sloper and Morris's sister. In the novel it occurs as part of the doctor's conscientious attempt to reach certainty about the young man's character. Though he never doubts the accuracy of his diagnosis, he wants to exorcise completely the possibility that Morris really is the one in twenty who defeats his well-honed expertise in human affairs no less than in medicine. He therefore visits Mrs. Montgomery in her modest abode. With remarkable honesty and sensitivity about the woman's reluctance to say anything ill about her brother, Sloper leads her to aver the selfishness in Morris, his duplicity in pretending that he tutors her children (except in teaching them Spanish), and his misrepresentation of how greatly he is depending on her meager income. At last, after Sloper has described Catherine as a girl who is ill-equipped to protect herself from that kind of man, Mrs. Montgomery bursts into tears and blurts out: "Don't let her marry him!"[13]

This is all the doctor needs to hear. It confirms not only his suspicions but also those of James and his readers. That then becomes a ruling principle in the novel. It is a fact of life that many men are erotic swindlers, on a par with women who employ their sexual powers to seduce men for monetary gain. Western fiction is filled with portrayals of both types of moral deceit. But Wyler's film, like the Goetzes' play, does not belong to that genre. It adheres to Jamesian ambiguity more consistently than James himself did in this novel.

As if to reinforce Mrs. Kemble's negative view of her brother, James transfers her words—slightly edited—to Mrs. Almond in the story. Having at first suspended judgment about Morris as a possible husband, Mrs. Almond changes her opinion after learning what Mrs. Montgomery has said to Sloper. As my readers will remember, Mrs. Kemble had told Miss T. : "If your father does relent and you are well off, he [her brother Henry] will make you a kindly enough husband, so long as all goes well. But if he should not, and you were to be poor, your lot would be miserable. *Then* my brother. . . would visit upon you his disappointment and discontent." The words that James puts into Mrs. Almond's mouth are the following: "If he marries her, and she comes into Austin's money, they may get on. He will be an idle, amiable, selfish, and, doubtless, tolerably good-natured fellow. But if she doesn't get the money, and he finds himself tied to her, heaven have mercy on her! He will have none. He will hate her for his disappointment, and take his revenge; he will be pitiless and cruel."[14]

In the Goetzes' play and in Wyler's movie, Sloper's meeting with Mrs. Montgomery is wholly revised and Mrs. Almond's judgment about Morris remains balanced and indecisive. In both the play and the movie, the meeting occurs at the doctor's home, not at Mrs. Montgomery's. This enables Mrs. Montgomery to see Catherine, who is extremely shy and socially somewhat gauche, just as her father portrayed her. But though Mrs. Montgomery recognizes the problem and sympathizes with the young woman, she resists the doctor's attempt to make her confirm his beliefs about the prejudicial selfishness of her brother. In contrast with the damaging words that finally issue from her in the novel, she moralistically tells the doctor that he expects too much of people and mistakenly thinks he or anyone else can see into a person's heart. The ambiguity of her remarks contributes to the dramatic texture of the film inasmuch as it prolongs the viewer's ongoing suspense about her brother's character.

As a result, our feelings toward Wyler's Morris continue to alternate, which they do systematically from the first time we see him until the very last shot. The first time we are shown only his back as he stands before Catherine, who is seated and to whom he is presenting himself. He thus appears to us as an expanse of darkness, his black formal attire excluding virtually everything else in the frame. That immediately creates in us a feeling of ominous apprehension, which is quickly dispelled when we then see how bright and handsome the stranger seems to be. In the last shot, our hearts go out to this man who is being mercilessly punished by the revenge that Catherine wreaks upon him. He is now standing in the darkness, not creating it by crowding out the light, and his piteous suffering as he bangs uncontrollably on the outside door in the fruitless hope that Catherine will open it stamps him as a victim and not just a ruthlessly aggressive male.

In the Holland movie, the meeting between Sloper and Morris's sister differs entirely from the previous versions. In various details Holland's scenario stays much closer to the novel than Wyler's or the play's. But in this important segment, it deviates considerably. As Wyler depicts her, Mrs. Montgomery is a modest and sympathetic woman in her middle years. Holland turns her into a person who is not only ten or fifteen years younger but also alert and liberated in a twentieth-century manner. She meets with Sloper in her squalid house through which her noisy children run about and quarrel with each other.

If the character in Wyler strikes us as a widow who courageously makes do on her own, the one in Holland seems like a strongminded and embittered single mother who expects to receive from the wealthy Sloper little understanding of what she confronts in life. She has no desire to assist him in his investigation. When he offers to help her financially if she and her children are deprived of the many benefits that might accrue to them from a marriage between Morris and his daughter, she loses her temper. Where the mousy Mrs. Montgomery in the novel quietly takes this offer into consideration though not overtly revealing its attractiveness, the militant young mother in the Holland movie is insulted by its mere suggestion. She orders Sloper out of her house, and men as well as women in the audience feel instinctively disgusted by his heartless behavior. In itself it keeps us from siding with his emphatic assurance that Morris is simply mercenary.

In other scenes Holland retains the Jamesian perspective more consistently than James himself. At one point she provides an elaboration of it that penetrates to the philosophical underpinnings of the story with more understanding than any of her forerunners, including James. Her doing so serves to compensate for her deletion of anything like the powerful sequence during which Wyler's Catherine waits in vain for Morris to fetch her on the night of her return from Europe. We see her there in terrible distress, and we intuit what she must feel in suspecting that Morris has abandoned her. Having eliminated that, Holland has Catherine chase after him on the morning of his departure from New York, allegedly on a business trip. It is now clear to Catherine that Morris is breaking off their relationship. Contrary to what is deemed proper behavior, she confronts him at his sister's house and begs him to tell her whether the loss of her father's legacy has precipitated his flight.

Morris evades the question at first, but then she demands that he say as much, so that she will not blame herself for having done something wrong. In reply he screams: "Say what? . . . That I wanted you with your money? Is that so immoral! Would you want me without my attributes? You have money; I have this. It was a fair exchange." When he flees into the street to take a cab that is waiting for him, Catherine wildly follows after. She catches up with him in a narrow passage that shields them from the pouring rain. She details how good a wife she would be and swallows whatever is left of her pride by tearfully insisting that the ten thousand dollars a year she brings on her own without her father's money is itself a fortune. In his tortured state, Morris shouts: "Not when one was expecting thirty and spent two years of one's youth in pursuance of it."

This sequence in Holland's movie ends with Catherine running after the cab and falling flat on her face in the muddy street. It is brilliant filmmaking, and nothing comparable exists in any other version. It is a dramatic counterpoint to the comic shots of Charles Pike falling in the mud after he gets off the train in *The Lady Eve* and Fredrik Egerman falling in the mud before entering Desirée's apartment house in Ingmar Bergman's *Smiles of a Summer Night*. What I find most remarkable, however, is the fact that the exchange between Catherine and Morris articulates problems in the philosophy of love that neither James nor Wyler and the Goetzes could handle with such expertise. The question of the money is common to the mythic theme they all deal with, but the nature of Morris's concern about it remains throughout what Hitchcock would call the "MacGuffin" in the plot. It is the unknown that feeds our suspense from scene to scene. In giving Morris the words that I have just quoted, Holland may seem to have aligned herself with James's narrator, like him seeing Morris as someone who cares about Catherine not for herself but only as a vehicle to the family fortune he is striving to possess. At the same time only Holland, in this speech, delves into and brings to the surface the pervasive ambiguity surrounding Morris.

In Wyler's version Lavinia defends Morris's acquisitiveness as a natural interest that any full-blooded male would have. She shocks Catherine by lamenting her having told Morris that they must not count on ever getting her father's twenty thousand dollars a year. When Catherine rejects what her aunt has said, in view of the ten thousand they will have in any event, that being a great deal of money, Lavinia replies: "Not when you have expected thirty." The Holland version goes beyond this.

In its own manner, the Goetzes' play does as well to some extent. At the beginning of the second act, Morris asks Lavinia whether Sloper will possibly disinherit Catherine if she marries him. When she reminds him that Catherine will still have her own ten thousand a year, Morris answers: "That would be small comfort. . . . On ten, ma'am, you live like your neighbor. . . . But thirty is something to look forward to. On thirty you live—(*His hand takes in the room*) like this." Lavinia remarks that he likes the house, and he agrees: "From the first evening that I was brought here, I have admired it, and all the things in it. The Doctor is a man of fine taste." Lavinia suggests that Morris is "more appreciative" than her brother, as also indicated by his response to Catherine's "true worth." "Yes, Catherine," Morris says casually as he handles a wine glass. "But also other things. For instance this crystal—it's Venetian."[15] These lines have been excised in the making of Wyler's film. By so greatly strengthening our suspicions about Morris, they would have weakened the ambivalence Wyler was carefully developing.

To clarify what I mean, I revert to the distinction I have studied in earlier writings about the roles of appraisal and bestowal in love as a whole. On my analysis they are both needed for love to occur. Through bestowal the lover creates a value in the beloved that does not exist otherwise but comes into being as a result of the imaginative acceptance of another as the person he or she is in him- or herself. By virtue of this affective attachment, the beloved achieves an importance over and above any that can be ascribed to desirable qualities apart from the relationship. Through appraisal, as it detects what can further our self-interest and satisfy whatever instinctual drives we may have innately, we crave objects and their attributes that will gratify our needs. Some of them are treated as objectively valuable since they yield goods that many in our society desire; others are individually valuable as relevant to what we want for ourselves in particular. Without appraisal, there could be no bestowal. Without bestowal, there would be no love as we know it. The two cooperate in the great disparity of interpersonal ideals that matter to human beings.

All this underlies Morris's speech in the Holland film as he tries to justify his freeing himself from Catherine's unwavering expectation. In saying there was a fair exchange in his offering his personal attributes—his wit and charm and physical appeal—while she embodied the goodness of great wealth, he is calling attention to the fact that love is not a matter of pure bestowal. It is instead dependent on equally operative appraisive values without which there can be no authentic love, but only a delusory attitude that brings misery to people who rely exclusively upon the undue occurrence of bestowal. In all the versions and from the very beginning, Sloper claimed that Catherine had to be protected from the allurement of falling in love with someone like Morris because it was not based on facts that the doctor perceived and she did not. The speech that Holland gives to Morris highlights what these facts are in this circumstance.

At this point and in this version, Morris admits his mercenary intentions. He also tells Catherine that she must forget him because, as he says appraisively, "I am not good enough." In other words, her generous ability to bestow exceptional value upon him is an unfortunate overvaluation, as Freud and Sloper would say. His incapacity to bestow love upon her under the actual circumstances may indeed be proof that he is not "good enough." But even so, his statement is based on an accurate estimate of what she is worth to him in view of her failing to deliver the thirty thousand dollars he had been seeking all along.

In Wyler's movie, before having concluded that Catherine would risk an eventual life of unhappiness if she married Morris, Mrs. Almond reasons with her brother that the likelihood of Morris being mercenary does not rule out the possibility of his becoming a good husband for her. "Be very careful, Austin," she urges, "This man may take care of Catherine *and* her money." To say that is to express the hope that appraisal and bestowal can be harmoniously united in a relationship—a marital one, in this case—that need not be totally selfish. The doctor's refusal to believe that Morris's character is such as to lend itself to this possibility propels the narrative to its variable conclusion—bleak in the Goetz play and their scenario for the Wyler film; affirmative, and even optimistic, in Holland's; and something in between in James's novel.

In probing the reasons for this differentiation among the endings, one must consider further the function the Don Juan myth and others play in both the cinematic and literary employment of the principal theme. The Wyler/Goetz version duplicates almost word for word the Jamesian verbal duel between Sloper and Morris in the scene where the doctor informs the young man that he does not belong to the category in which a plausible suitor belongs. When Catherine intervenes and the father offers to take her to Europe for a long stay designed to cure her infatuation, Morris convinces her to agree. He does not do so in the novel. In the film it causes us to think at that juncture that he may not be interested in only the money. This equilibration endures while she is in Europe and the two lovers exchange ardent letters. Once Morris runs away instead of eloping with Catherine upon her return, the doctor would seem to have won the duel. He tells Catherine this event proves that Morris never did love her, and she answers that she knows it now. But then, and earlier when she decides to elope, Wyler augments the Jamesian drama by turning Catherine into a duelist with her father in the place of Morris. The father has not won; he has merely created a more virulent adversary in the daughter he was trying to protect.

In this respect the Don Juan motif in Wyler's mythology evolves into a variation that exceeds any of its traditional predecessors. It is as if Donna Anna in Mozart's libretto has venomously turned upon the Commendatore because he disapproved of her cavorting—though only as a victim—with the Don Juan who sought sexual intercourse with her. Though she continues to live at home, Catherine vents her hatred upon her father in the powerful scene in which she condemns him not only for failing to love her himself but also for preventing her from marrying Morris whom she loves whether or not he reciprocates.

As it generally does, Holland's version remains closer to its origin in the Jamesian text. We see Catherine working in the kitchen and preparing her father's meal just after Morris has deserted her. When the old man has his stroke, she hurries to his aid. In his subsequent debility, she devotedly spoonfeeds him in bed. During the scene in which the lawyer reads the last will and testament shortly afterward, she is dressed in conventional mourning black and refuses to contest her father's final decision to donate his wealth, except for the house in Washington Square, to worthy charities. Goetz / Wyler's version had altered that provision in the will, giving Catherine the larger sum that Morris anticipated, but Holland's retains her partial disinheritance as in the novel.

The Wyler movie was released in 1949, just after the World War II period in which females entered the economy as never before. The men were in the armed forces, and many women at home realized that they were capable of doing jobs in the factories, even as welders, from which they had always been excluded. Though *The Heiress* purports to be about life a hundred years earlier, it responds and also contributes to the phase of the women's liberation movement that existed at the time. Catherine's hostility toward the tyrannical patriarch who has ruined her life is so powerful that she glumly waits outside in the park and rejects his plea for her to be with him when he dies. Instead of maintaining the storyline in which Catherine's submissiveness and filial dedication remain despite the harm her father has done to her, Wyler's shifting from the duel between Morris and Sloper to the emerging and combative strength of Catherine in opposition to her father creates an overarching rhythm that has a dramatic tension of its own. The greatness of the film largely results from that.

This change of focus also induces an additional ambiguity. From having elicited our suspenseful uncertainty about Morris's character, Wyler concludes with a depiction of the moral, though deadly, reverberation in Catherine. Grappling with Sloper as male to male in a delicate situation that requires a show of suavity and acceptance of social proprieties, Morris is scrupulously polite in his argumentation. But once he has removed himself as the prime antagonist and Catherine takes his place, we see the anger and wounded ugliness in her personality that emerges as a repudiation of the mildness and purity of heart that she had shown until then.

We have in stock wise saws such as "Hell hath no fury like a woman scorned" or the implication of King Lear's self-pitying remark "How sharper than a serpent's tooth is the tongue of a thankless child." But the animosity in Wyler's Catherine exceeds them both. Having won her duel with her father, in the sense that he dies a little later and she is unrelenting until he does, Catherine turns her well-honed weapons upon Morris when he reappears. He has come back virtually defeated in the life he has tried to pursue in the west. He begs for her mercy and understanding. She lures him into believing she will marry him now that her father is gone and she has inherited all his money. As he then discovers, she has only been setting him up for torture.

Olivia de Havilland acts out the ghastly deception beautifully. Though she deftly fools the audience in the process of fooling Morris, once she has snapped the trap we realize her gestures in responding to him were so artfully nuanced that neither he nor we could know she does not have loving or even humane feelings toward him. As the Italian saying goes: "Revenge is a dish that must be eaten cold." In his villainy that is the principle Iago subscribes to as a means of expressing his hatred toward Othello. In relation to Catherine, we are shocked that this likable woman, whose developing character we have been watching with a sympathetic hope that she will eventually attain the goodness of fulfilled desire and mutual love, should now have turned into a vicious destroyer of someone who promises to love her better than he did before. When Aunt Lavinia learns what is happening, she says to her: "Oh, can you be so cruel?" To which Catherine replies with frigidity: "Yes, Aunt, I can. I have been taught by masters." We can only shudder at the profound and previously hidden regions of her mind in which this corrupt education by her masters must have been lurking.

The Wyler version is a tragedy, as I suggested, because the ideal possibilities of marriage, which are interpersonal love and familial happiness that can burgeon from it, have been destroyed by the social ugliness of monetary greed, parental domination, and filial hostility. In the last shots, Catherine holds her candle as she goes upstairs into the darkness beyond as if she were walking into her grave. On her face is a slight look of relief that her affective problem has finally been resolved, or rather bypassed, but her countenance also instills in us a sense that Catherine's life is finished now. We have heard of no other suitors, though James had suggested that some existed. Given the modesty and reserve that we perceived in her at the outset, we cannot imagine that she will allow herself to run the risk of repeating her harrowing experience. All the joy and all the suffering of love is ended for her, and that alone is her tragedy.

The tragedy of Morris is of a related yet different kind. Copland's loud and frantic music augments the furious sounds of Morris's pounding on the door even after he realizes from the reflected light of Catherine's candle as it rises upon the stairs that she will not let him in. Having been misled by her deceptiveness to believe that she would forgive him and allow him to mend his former behavior—in other words, that they can somehow live together in marital love—he is incapable of accepting his conclusive dismissal.

After Catherine had asked Morris to wait while she brings down her wedding gift for him, he looks about the sumptuous house and happily tells Lavinia: "I'm home! I'm really home!" He means the residence he previously wanted, possibly more than he wanted Catherine. But now his basic impulse is explicated through the concept of "home." Every male yearns to return there in some fashion, and the woman he marries brings with her a mythic womb that itself symbolizes the home from which her suitor came and may reenter under the altered conditions of normal heterosexuality. Morris's terminal exclusion reverberates with the tragedy Adam undergoes when he is thrust out of Eden. At stake is more than just rectifying the moral flaw referred to in *Hamlet*. It is also the danger of death-in-life that we all must face throughout our existence. Being star-crossed lovers, Catherine and Morris are each doomed to that painful outcome.

In its preparation for this denouement, Wyler's camera continually focuses upon views of the fine house in which Morris had cultivated his fantasy of a home for himself. As the habitat of the material goodness that Morris craves, and the Slopers take for granted, the interior becomes a virtual character in the overall story. The angles at which we see Catherine walk, and sometimes run, upstairs or down establish a rhythm of their own. What happens in the front and back parlors is augmented by their spacious openness and dark wood paneling that bespeak the opulence of the place. The closing of the mahogany double doors that lead to the drawing room in which Sloper duels with Morris provides a suitable introduction to that event.

Wyler's inspired use of mirrors in the house serves a double function. By reflecting back into the rooms in which they are located, they enlarge the visual space that the film audience can observe. That adds to the importance of what is being enacted.

But also, in one pivotal sequence, the well-positioned mirror makes a cinematographic comment that is more telling than any verbal description could be. When the father comes downstairs from his sickbed and discovers Catherine at her loom a few days after they have returned from abroad, she will not talk to him face to face at first. She answers his questioning by talking to the mirror before which she is seated and in which she can see his reflection. It is a device that enables her to control her anger while also asserting that he no longer exists for her.

Earlier Catherine told Morris, and then Lavinia, that she wanted to elope with him so that she would never have to be in that house and see her odious father there again. When she finally turns around on this occasion and looks him in the eye, she verbally attacks Sloper in an enflamed voice she never had before. It all happens in the same place, but the presence and appearance of the house, through the mirrors and apart from them as well, vary in conformity with the human feelings that occur in this locale from scene to scene. In the film's last shots, the building's tall front doors defy and forever exclude the would-be husband who is pounding menacingly on them.[16]

Though Holland's film is not a tragedy, it is certainly not a romance that concludes with well-appointed lovers joining hands and living happily ever after. Nevertheless, it is affirmative in the sense that it portrays the awakening of a troubled young woman who ultimately rises above her excessive dependence upon an arrogant and demanding father as well as her fate in growing up without a mother. As a girl, Holland's Catherine is socially unstable and occasionally zany, but the great attention bestowed by so handsome and elegant a man as

Morris registers upon her in a very beneficial way. By the end of the movie, she is fully in control of her destiny as someone who does not have to have the affiliation of either a husband or a demonstrative lover. She can manage very well by herself.

Wyler's Catherine is never a troubled person, just a shy and backward one in the presence of strangers, yet also perceptive and sometimes witty. She too attains greater self-composure, though, unlike the Catherine in Holland's adaptation, she does not reach a satisfying solution to her former problems. While she has wealth and belongs to a small society of like-minded people, she has no vital role in the world she inhabits. She is more like the Catherine in James's novel in that respect.

In Wyler's movie we scarcely see the lovers doing much of anything together. The piano on which Morris plays the "plaisirs d'amour" music is used only that one time and by him alone: Catherine, in contrast to her mother, is said not to have "a true ear." Holland gives her that, and the early rapport between Catherine and Morris is displayed in the duet they perform together in front of her family. It is an Italian song in which the two pianists also sing responsively to each other. At the end of the movie, Catherine plays the piano for a large number of small children who are gathered together in her living room and who sing along with her. She is happy in their midst. When they leave, Morris appears after his years of absence. He is meek and apologetic, and Catherine is completely in charge. She is polite and kindly disposed toward him, but filled with neither love nor hatred. When he asks whether they can be friends after all, she tells him not to come again. She obviously has matured as a human being who has found that her affection for the children she spends her time with is quite sufficient for her emotional requirements.

Previously, when her father was alive, we saw her converse with a fine-looking suitor. She did not encourage his matrimonial advances, but we imagine that she might change her mind. Having spoken to Morris again, and presumably for the last time, anything seems possible for her in her developed condition of self-assurance. As she thinks about Morris's visit, the background music softly reiterates a portion of the Italian song that she and he had played together. She idly fingers it on the piano herself, but then the voice of a trained singer, an accomplished vocalist, takes over. The woman's resonant tones are those of a person who can express her feelings by performing them alone, not in a duet with a man as the song was originally presented. The last shot of Catherine shows her nodding inwardly and smiling slightly as she thinks of her success in have moved beyond the Morris chapter in her life. It is as if she were saying to herself: "Well, I've had the experience. I have known what it is to be in love, the pleasures and the sorrows. I can now devote myself to the other things that life might offer, the other ways in which I may yet have a happy and meaningful existence."

But does her calm and even serene demeanor indicate a willingness to seek romantic fulfillment with some new individual who will cross her path? There is no need for Holland to answer that question. Instead she has one of the young girls who was singing in the group return to the living room and embrace Catherine as a teacher or surrogate mother she adores. Catherine told Morris she suffered greatly for three years after he abandoned her. It is clear that she, unlike her namesake in Wyler, we surmise, has long since got over that.

For his part James does not take the story that far, though in the novel the older Catherine and Morris are not tragic either. When he seeks her out after the years have passed, he is a world-weary person who expects very little out of life. James says he is paunchy and middle-aged. We are told that Catherine lives comfortably in the family house and on the enlarged inheritance Morris coveted, but that her activities in the world are limited and unexciting. She performs her social and charitable duties in keeping with her affluent lifestyle, and that suffices for a pleasant and respectable life. As a child and young woman, she is described by James as mentally slow and unimpressive—even backward, her father continually insists. During her torrid love affair, she comes alive and shows real emotion that surprises him. But after she has survived her disappointment and humiliation, she reverts to her former, more or less passive, state of being. In his anti-Romantic recitation, James obviously wants us to believe that this represents the existence of rich New Yorkers who lived in the moment of American capitalism he is realistically documenting.

Despite the nineteenth-century clothing and period settings, Holland's movie is not only addressed to a present-day audience but also includes systematic access to current taste in what can be seen and said on screen. After the coy and unexplicit mention of private endearments that the lovers exchange on one occasion, James seems to titter as he withdraws and allows the reader to imagine the rest. Wyler allows them to kiss only when they declare and then reiterate their desire to wed, though after Catherine returns from Europe the two embrace ecstatically in the driving rain and under the downpour of Copland's oceanic renewal of the "plaisirs d'amour" music. That, however, is all we see. The dramatic propulsion of the movie and the play does not permit more overt demonstration of what young lovers might be doing in each other's company in 1860. The type of realism that Holland imposes, however, continually demands sexual displays that viewers in our decade expect to find in the films they frequent. Her movie fulfills this imperative.

For one thing, there are quite a few scenes in which the lovers carry on as youngsters often do nowadays in rooms of the paternal home while no one can watch them. Catherine and Morris kiss and grope each other fervently, slide down to the floor together, and act as if they might—though they do not—begin to remove each other's clothing. We are used to that in a love story, and of course Holland is free to render hers in this or any other manner. Still, there are touches of cinematic grandeur that appear in Wyler's version that she cannot approach as a result of her more explicit presentation. For instance, when Wyler's Catherine is first flushed with the excitement of Morris's proposal of marriage and the love language he uses to convince her that his feelings are authentic, she melts in his arms and at one point buries her face in the broad lapel of his jacket. A little later, after she has kissed him on the lips, she even kisses it. The gesture expresses her unspeakable joy in having entered into an amatory relationship with a real man, a male who knows how to dress well and how to charm a young woman like herself.

This slight but significant effect is one among others that Wyler's cinematography employs to express the ideas he is working with. In this case they involve the question about appraisal and bestowal that I referred to previously. Throughout all of the five versions, Catherine is portrayed not only as a woman in love but also as a woman whose love is at first true and entirely untainted. But does that mean, as a long tradition in the philosophy of love maintains, that her love is selfless, inherently sacrificial, and a total bestowal of oneself without any concern for personal recompense?

The Morris in Holland's film is emotionally distraught and almost out of control when he speaks the lines I have quoted about the "fair exchange" between the goods that Catherine receives from him and the money he has hoped to get through her. This is the truth that dare not speak its name, since it discloses the impurity in all attachments of a romantic sort. Without addressing the issue as Holland does, Wyler's shot of Catherine burying her face in Morris's jacket signifies everything of goodness and instinctual delight that she craves as any woman in love naturally would. Because that is so commonplace a joy, and so often sought, Wyler's artful technique is able to arouse in us the sadness we feel when it is plowed under by the conflict between the two aggressive men in Catherine's life.

In being a recent work and therefore more sensationalistic than its predecessor, Holland's version expands the narrative to include scenes that neither James nor Wyler could accommodate. In the Holland movie, when Lavinia tells Morris they must meet secretly in order to make plans, he chooses a rendezvous in a seedy and lower-class market area where no one can possibly recognize them. In her theatrical and overly Romantic fashion, Lavinia likes the suggestion. We see her wend her way through a noisy throng of rough-handed workmen. When she encounters Morris in a disreputable eating place, they sit at a small table next to a billowing curtain of flimsy gauze through which we hear the erotic banter of an unknown man and woman. As Morris and Lavinia talk to each other, the adjacent conversation becomes more and more erotic, and finally indicative of some form of sexual behavior being vigorously performed. Lavinia is disconcerted by this and asks, whimsically but also as proof of her inability to understand what happens between men and women: "What are they doing in there?" In character, Morris blandly replies: "I have no idea."

The foolishness of Lavinia is a constant in all the literary and cinematic variants. As a person of dubious judgment, she arises out of Mrs. Kemble's brief mention of her sister Mrs. S., who tries to reunite Miss T. with the treacherous brother. In James, Lavinia's siblings, Sloper and Mrs. Almond, both ridicule her silly romanticism as well as her uncanny ability to wreck any venture she seeks to aid. The doctor's repugnance toward Lavinia appears throughout the novel, and in one place he tells Mrs. Almond that he is glad Lavinia "is not on my side; she is capable of ruining an excellent cause. The day Lavinia gets into your boat it capsizes."[17]

James himself adds his own ironic touch when he speaks of Lavinia's "restless brain," her "powerful" imagination, and her undying faith in what she calls Morris's "scruples" in separating from Catherine as he did. Wyler's Catherine mocks her time and again. When Catherine is preparing for what she thinks will be her elopement with Morris in the middle of the night, Lavinia exults at the beauty of that and exclaims: "Oh, I hope I will always be romantic." At this point her wild enthusiasm has possibly infected Catherine as well, but it is only she who has to experience the fearful consequences of this ideology when Morris does not show up.

In Holland's film, Lavinia's intrusion into Catherine's affairs becomes even more evident than in Wyler's. James had intimated that Lavinia's affection for Morris went beyond any dispassionate appreciation of his merits as a possible mate for Catherine. She herself admits that she has come to feel toward him as if he were a son of hers. While Sloper and Catherine are in Europe she gives Morris the run of the house as a highly honored guest and companion. Wyler emphasizes his self-indulgent acceptance of Lavinia's kindness. It leads into Sloper's fury when he returns and has to face the fact that Morris has, as he intimates, used his house as a private club.

To all this, Holland adds an effective touch that reveals how greatly Catherine has developed into an emotionally mature woman. After her stay abroad, she looks and acts like a person who is virtually married already and soon to have her legal wedding. She lashes out at Lavinia for having used her absence as a means of trying to steal Morris's affections, as only a surrogate son perhaps but also as a likely figment of her invidious imagining about his erotic intimacy with herself.

Being the character who bears this medley of unwholesome characteristics, Lavinia embodies everything that James finds repulsive in the Romantic literature of his age. In all of the versions we find Catherine coping somehow with the shortcomings of the reigning romanticism. Neither James nor the others indicate which mythology would be preferable to it. But do they need to? At least from an aesthetic point of view, what they provide with much success is surely sufficient in itself.

In the trajectory of her characterization from James to Wyler and then to Holland, Catherine manifests the myth of Dido and Aeneas in variable fashion. In the Virgil original, the goodhearted queen suffers to the point of suicide when the hero she passionately loves deserts her. He goes off in conformance to a masculine myth of military conquest and nation building for which the gods have chosen him. Though Dido has already proven herself a strong and wise ruler of her people, the personal loss is too great for her to surmount. She thereby embodies the mythology of the suffering female in love that recurs throughout Western literature. In most cases, as in Catherine's, the abandoned female does not kill herself. But the anguish of these women is very great, and, like Catherine in Wyler's film, they frequently have to accept an emotional death-in-life that anticipates their actual demise.

By the time we get to the nineteenth century, however, the now-emancipated female is often morally stronger than the male, after he leaves her as well as before. That is the theme in Hector Berlioz's opera *Les Troyens*, which is a retelling of Virgil's story of Dido and Aeneas. It is a supreme examplar of nineteenth-century romanticism in its feminist mode. Though Berlioz's Didon dies as required by the legend, she does so as a regal person far superior to the lover who sneaks away. In Holland's movie she is reborn in the Catherine who seemed so pitiful at the beginning but ends up having risen, even blossomed, by courageously dealing with the sorrows of her ill-fated romance.

In this re-creation, Holland's cinematic mythmaking illumines all the Jamesian heroines who suffer as Catherine does but come out victorious in alternate responses that basically resemble hers. I am thinking in particular of Isabel Archer in *The Portrait of a Lady*, Milly Theale in *The Wings of the Dove*, and Maggie Verver in *The Golden Bowl*. These three novels have recently been made into accomplished movies. Like *The Heiress* and *Washington Square*, they attest to the unremitting validity of the Dido myth in our mentality alongside the other myths of love we have been discussing.

In the 2005 film *Proof,* the main character, also named Catherine, reenacts the mythic ambivalence in Holland's protagonist. She exists in present-day Chicago and is the devoted daughter of a mathematical genius, whose exceptional powers she has inherited, though possibly also his insanity or rational debility in the years before he died. Like the others in the myth, she is a troubled female whose excessive love for her father has caused not only her psychological distress but also her uncertainty about her ability to excel as a mathematician. The Morris Townsend type of young man who comes into her life tries to convince her that a notebook containing a revolutionary achievement in the field is her own work, not just a copy of what her father may have written in his terminal period of madness.

Proof has a happy ending inasmuch as the young man never deserts Catherine and ultimately unites with her as an intimate companion. In a scene that reverses the climactic one in Holland's film that ends with Catherine in the mud, this substitute for Morris runs after her car and flings back to her the crucial notebook she had discarded as worthless. The last frames of *Proof* go beyond the mildly feminist culmination of Holland's *Washington Square.* They show Catherine collaborating with her suitor in a manner that reveals not only her capacity for sexual oneness but also her acceptance of her indubitable eminence in creative mathematics. This renders the mythology utterly modern.

4

Cocteau: The Mythological Poetry of Film

Jean Cocteau differed from other filmmakers in two respects. He approached cinema as a form of poetry, and the majority of the relatively few films he made or wrote were explicitly mythological. Many filmmakers have aspired to a poetic dimension beyond or within the realistic fabric of their movies. Yet hardly any of them was an accomplished and talented poet, as Cocteau was; and few have developed an aesthetics of film *as* poetry that is comparable to what exists in his theoretical writings. Even Welles and Renoir, both of whom were greater filmmakers than Cocteau, mention in an offhanded way the poetic elements that lurk within their naturalistic images. But neither does much to clarify these casual statements. More than Welles or Renoir, Cocteau creates images that are visual equivalents to the figurative devices that distinguish written poetry from prose. For him cinema is a modern extension through different technology of what poetry has been attempting all along. His reliance upon the fertile meaningfulness of classical mythology issues organically out of that conception.

To people who lived in ancient Greece or medieval Europe, or even Western countries in the modern world, the myths and enacted ceremonies of their times may often have retained some resonance of literal truth. In the experience of those individuals, whose number is immeasurable, mythology was more than just an aesthetic communication of attitudes and ideals embodied in engaging stories. What nowadays seems fanciful or magical, and therefore merely imaginative, was often taken as an appropriate revelation of what science and the superscience of religion might ultimately disclose. Cocteau reverses that perspective. For him the ordinary world is *in itself* a phantasy, an artifact of magic beyond the comprehension of any science. By depicting realistically the arcane inventions of his imagination, in poetry or film or, for that matter, painting and sculpture, he thought he could reveal the inner dimensions of the world we consider ordinary.

The mythology Cocteau conveys and embellishes with great originality is not designed to raise the audience to some lofty realm, or in general to liberate it from the harsh realities of factual existence. He takes the mission of poetry to be an artistic cleansing of our immersion in life tantamount to the restoration of a soiled or damaged portrait. It is neither a divertissement nor proof of empirical certitudes, but rather the showing forth of a reality that resides in some entrancing and well-contrived fable. In film that approach issues into visual narratives (or quasi-narratives) that exceed the limits of the written word. In their structured impact, the cinematic effects are nevertheless kindred to what appears in the art of poetry.

Coherent with this, Cocteau distinguishes between the poetry of film and what most people deem "poetic." The latter is a kind of verbal posturing, he says, and therefore boring. It lacquers over an empty imagination instead of penetrating to what we experience but cannot otherwise express adequately. Moreover, the so-called poetic manifests a studied attempt to be or seem original, whereas in films such as his the poetry is "incidental" and produced unconsciously: "A great number of excursions into the poetic contain not the slightest poetry. On the other hand there are realistic ventures which radiate a poetry that bathes them in phosphorescent light."[1]

What Cocteau refers to as unconscious is not the same as the Freudian construct. It is a state *between* slumber and daytime alertness needed for survival. The poet or filmmaker like himself is half-awake, but neither prone to daydreaming nor trying to display the content or import of actual dreams. On the contrary, Cocteau insists, the poetry in film evokes in its proper audience a response that is closer to hypnosis than to dreaming of the usual sort:

> A film is not the telling of a dream, but a dream in which we all participate together through a kind of hypnosis, and the slightest breakdown in the mechanics of the dream wakens the dreamer, who loses interest in a sleep that is no longer his own.
>
> By dream, I mean a succession of real events that follow on from one another with the magnificent absurdity of dreams, since the spectators would not have linked them together in the same way or have imagined them for themselves, but experience them in their seats as they might experience, in their beds, strange adventures for which they are not responsible.[2]

The crucial emphasis in this quote consists in Cocteau's claim, often repeated, that his films address the poetry inherent in real events, which may resemble the kind of dreaming that Freud and the Freudians investigate but only in having the "magnificent absurdity" that belongs to each.

In a similar vein Cocteau repudiated the aesthetics of surrealism with which his work was commonly associated. Critics of

The Blood of a Poet (1930) scorned the film as merely derivative from what Salvador Dalí and Luis Buñuel had already done in *Un chien andalou*, released shortly before. There are indeed borrowings from that earlier work, and Cocteau's idea of a mouth in a drawing being transferred to the painter's hand when he erases it may have borrowed from the erasing of a man's mouth in *Un chien andalou* when he rubs it, the hair from a woman's armpit then sprouting in that part of his face.

All this intriguing nonsense arrests attention as it should, and as it does at the very beginning of *Un chien andalou* with the crude but still magical slitting of the woman's eye. But having digested the cleverness in this kind of technique, Cocteau deploys it in a creative fashion that goes far beyond surrealism. He uses the contrivance of a mouth that moves and even talks from within the painter's hand as a vehicle for exploring the hazards in all aesthetic emanations from oneself that are put into some external object—a drawing or a poem or any other artistic entity that is capable of showing what its creator is. Moreover, Cocteau's exploration occurs within a social order, specifically one that is disintegrating, as indicated in *The Blood of a Poet* by the tall chimney that buckles at the beginning and finally falls to the ground at the end.

These images that Cocteau flashes before us are not presented as symbols that one might interpret in the systematic manner of dream or other psychiatric analysis. Cocteau rightly ridicules the belief by "300 girls from a Catholic Psychoanalytic Institute" that the crumbling chimney is a phallic symbol. He does not deny that once his work has been finished and offered to the public it can be experienced in a great variety of ways. But that applies to life in general, and Cocteau wisely remarks that what he or anyone else might say about the contents of his film can only be "a text written *after the fact*, after the images."[3] In making films, he sought only to film poetry itself. This meant being fully immersed in the expertise that combines visual and auditory effects, including music, and voyaging through the solitary and quasi-somnambulistic realm of imaginative possibilities that filmmakers inhabit just as poets do.

Cocteau gives a definitive statement of his view when he says that although *The Blood of a Poet* does not resort to dreams or even symbols, "it imitates their mechanism, rather, and by a certain relaxation of mind, like that of sleep, lets memories combine, maneuver, wander at will. As for symbols, the film avoids them, substituting actions or allegories of those actions, out of which the spectator can make up his own symbols, if he wants to."[4]

Time and again, Cocteau defines the role of the artist—not just the poet or the filmmaker, but other artists as well—as analogous to the work of a carpenter. Their art consists in making a table that is well constructed, firm, and solid. "The mediums come afterwards, and it is their business to make the tables talk."[5] This is not to say that the nature of art is misconstrued only by those who think that it must articulate spiritual and perhaps religious meanings that the artist intends to convey. In rejecting that kind of mindset, Cocteau is also attacking the rationalism that limits creative thinking about our life and behavior to the purely cognitive categories in which even existentialist philosophers of the twentieth and twenty-first centuries have been schooled. By addressing the netherworld between everyday consciousness and the dreamlike condition of one who sleeps, the mythological concepts Cocteau proffers defy the pretensions of reason as a final arbiter of knowledge and insight about the human condition.

Cocteau has often been treated as a dilettante or flimsy thinker by persons who fail to appreciate the importance of his panoramic efforts to deconstruct the dominant edifice of Western rationalism. In his own (relatively sympathetic) way, Jean-Paul Sartre was one of these dismissive people. A memento he published after Cocteau died reads as follows: "I greatly liked Cocteau, whom I knew in 1944, and whom I often saw until the end; I dined with him several days before his death. I found him very amiable, and much less of a clown than he is felt to be nowadays. It was he above all who did the talking. He spoke of his way of seeing the world, and his ideas—which I never followed more than a very little, since he was superficial, as it seemed to me. He was a very brilliant talker, he had plenty of sensibility, but few ideas. Which does not mean that I did not regard him as a poet of great value."[6]

In studying Cocteau's achievement as a mythmaker whose work elucidates the poetry of films, I hope to exceed the reach of Sartre's judgment.

A good starting point is *La Belle et la Bête* (1946), whose title I leave in French in order not to confuse it with Disney's *Beauty and the Beast*, made forty-five years later. Both films rely heavily on a reality in magic that contravenes our normal perception of reality. But since *Beauty and the Beast* is a feature-length cartoon, its patrons have submitted in advance to the prospect of an entire world and all the people in it being represented magically by a wandlike brush in the artist's hand. In *Fantasia* (1941) Mickey Mouse portrayed the luckless underling in *The Sorcerer's Apprentice*. So successful was he in that role that he himself became an icon of cartoonists and the other wondrous artisans who make animated films. To this day he still appears as the sorcerer himself, dressed in a wizard's conical hat and multicolored gown, and even enclosed within a semihalo that suggests his mystical status.

We in the audience of *Beauty and the Beast* are amused but not astounded when the candlestick Lumière speaks luminescently with a Gallic accent and with expressively accentuated eyebrows. His name means "light" in French, and it reminds us of the famous pioneer in filmmaking. It is a play of imagination similar to having the tea pitcher talk in the cultivated and domestic manner of an English housewife. We are not even shocked by the grotesque appearance of the Beast, at first hideously amorphous though soon to be seen wearing men's knee breeches and dancing shoes. We have been prepared for all that by the century of animation preceding it. Belle and her father are frightened by the possibility that the Beast will eat or otherwise harm them, as they also are in *La Belle et la Bête*, but the profundity that gives artistic sustenance to Cocteau's film is precluded from Disney's *Beauty and the Beast* by the simple-minded expectations inherent in the genre of the latter movie.

As Cocteau distinguished poetry from the merely poetic, so too can one explain the structure of his work in terms of the difference between magic and the magical. Disney's film is magical through and through, but Cocteau approaches the fable with a different outlook. He told Christian Bérard, who did the sets, and Henri Alekan, the cinematographer, that they were to capture *the reality of magic* rather than making reality look magical. He wanted a documentary of the enchanted castle as if it were another world that we can experience as directly as the one to which we are accustomed. For those in general who wish to make wonderful movies, Cocteau's advice was "Steer clear of magic."[7] He believed that the more a film is unreal, the more realism is needed in order for the audience to be convinced. One might say the same about poetry.

To carry out Cocteau's intention, most of *La Belle et la Bête* sustains an alternation, and even counterbalance, as Renoir would have called it, between two aspects of existence. One of them, presented first since that is the world the audience presupposes, consists of prosaic country life in seventeenth-century France. In the other, there lurk occult forces that belong to a level of being beyond anything we have seen in the routine circumstances of Belle and her family. The difference begins when the father comes upon the strange habitation in the middle of the forest. He had been afraid to go through the woods at night because he thought predatory animals might attack him. When he enters the castle and is later abused in perfect French by the ferocious Beast, he finds himself in another world entirely, a domain that is fearful in a deeper and more worrisome fashion than anything he foresaw.

In this world that astounds the father, and then Belle when she arrives in it, suspense is generated in us because—like them—we have no idea what to expect of its inherent reality. When the father reaches the outside door, his enormous shadow looms inexplicably in front of him, as if the laws of nature that exist in the previous scenes no longer operate. And indeed the doors open by themselves, presumably in response to the weight of the shadow that leans against them. In the empty corridor the human arms that come out of the walls holding lighted candelabras beckon forward in progressive unison, as if to signify that the father's arrival has somehow been anticipated by them.

We have no way of accounting for this or other marvels that appear once the father sits down at the dinner table—the caryatids, sculpted heads at either end of the mantelpiece who have eyes that peer from side to side and nostrils that emit puffs of smoke; the detached hand that pours the wine and invisibly serves the food that appears in front of the baffled man. Nor will any explanation be provided for all the other evidences of magic that Belle encounters later on, and repeatedly, prior to the final denouement that eventually terminates the mounting suspense we feel about the Beast and his fabulous residence.

Instead of introducing that kind of suspense, which is more mythological because more probing of reality, the Disney film relies upon the suspense that belongs to action films. In this one, the militant country folk, led by the self-centered male chauvinist who wants to take marital possession of Belle, are defeated by the animated utensils and accoutrements of the castle, after which the plot proceeds to show us how she and the Beast reach the matrimonial harmony that we have expected from the start. Though a moral verity proclaims itself in this, there is at no point any questioning about the relation between the real and unreal in what we are watching. The humor and romantic charm of Disney's distracting fantasy is entertaining for adults as well as children, but that is all that can be said about it.

Despite the fearfulness of the scenes in which the wolves attack the Disney Belle and her horse, and the depressed condition into which the Beast eventually descends, the animated film remains primarily farcical. Even the cataclysmic death of Gaston, the odious chauvinist, hardly seems worthy of much compassion. In Cocteau's film, the comedic element is concentrated in the early scenes that portray how ridiculous the arrogant and scheming sisters are, in contrast to their Cinderella sibling, and how little her suitor Avenant can match the purity of heart that characterizes Belle's universal love. When one of the sisters evicts a chicken who has been reposing in her sedan chair and the bird squeaks its disapproval, we laugh because the little beast expresses the contempt for the woman that we also feel. When Belle secretly mounts Magnifique, the magic horse who will take her to the castle instead of her father, we identify with her pristine act of filial love.

This contrast between the two realities having been established, the comedy in Cocteau's version then become a romance that ends with the tragic outcome of Avenant's authentic but sullied affection as well as the beginning of erotic happiness that awaits Belle and the princely Beast. In the gradual morph of Avenant after he has been shot by the offended goddess (Diana the virginal huntress whose sanctified pavilion Avenant has violated by smashing its glass ceiling, much as an invasive male might break a girl's maidenhead), we see the horror he feels as he himself turns into the Beast against whom he had wanted to defend the woman he loves.

Though we might think of this metamorphosis as the young man's punishment for coveting the treasure stored in the pavilion, his accomplice—Belle's brother—does not suffer a similar fate. He is allowed to run away unscathed. It is as if the passional bliss that Belle and her now unbestial Beast will henceforth experience must be paid for by the ritual substitution of another male whose base humanity can only be expunged by a renewal of the magic we have been watching. Cocteau invents the character of Avenant, as well as this adjunct to the traditional story. Nothing like it is to be found in the 1756 account by Madame Leprince de Beaumont that he drew upon selectively.

Two components of Cocteau's thinking enter into this elaboration: his sense of the radical imperfection and inevitable failing in all questing individuals; and his forceful longing for death that will liberate him into a transcendent, and hence mythological, reality that is foundational to the one we all encounter daily though it can be fully recognized only in poetry and the other arts. These major principles recur throughout Cocteau's films, but here I want to mention an instance of each. In *The Testament of Orpheus*, the explicitly autobiographical film that Cocteau made at the end of his life, the personage he projects while playing the role himself is likewise shot in the back by a goddess—this time Athena, who harpoons him for daring to approach her in his worthless condition. And in both of his Orphic films as well as *The Blood of a Poet*, the theme of mutual though unhappy love between the poet and the enigmatic Death who pursues him as much as he pursues her has central importance throughout Cocteau's mythology. In *La Belle et la Bête* this motif is less fully developed than in his other movies.

Returning briefly to the Disney production, we find one montage in it that emulates Cocteau's inventiveness. As a frontispiece, and as a restatement at the close, the animated film displays a vignette in frozen frame that is not itself animated but rather a photographic reproduction. It shows a tablet or multicolored stained-glass window that portrays the lovers in the fable. They are stylized and quaintly molded as if they come from a venerated era that guarantees their legendary value as aesthetic emblems. We see the handsome Prince in a white uniform, Belle serene and beautiful in a flowing white gown, and above them a big red rose that symbolizes the ardent and fully sexual goal that each of them seeks. There is a kind of poetry in this static picture, and its attempt to add generic prestige to the fable is acceptable as a claim to mythological validity. But Cocteau's imagination is more fertile than that. In his version, the rose the father finds and plucks for Belle, and because of which he nearly loses his life, is notably white and small rather than red and large.

Though not made in color, Cocteau's movie could have duplicated—scarcely but possibly—the redness of a red rose. It is nevertheless clear that the whiteness of the white rose that he prefers has a function of its own. The dramatic contrast between black and white is in fact part of the mythic orientation of his film. The Beast is dressed in sumptuous black until his fundamental goodness becomes manifest, and at the conclusion his attire is lustrous white; the father blunders upon the castle after losing his way at night in the obscurity of a storm-filled forest, and almost all the scenes at the castle take place in semidarkness until Belle arrives and with her purity of being whitens the place.

The significance of whiteness is accentuated by the scene in which Belle faints after seeing the frightful Beast for the first time. He picks her up and carries her in a fairly long sequence through the chiaroscuro of the castle, up the stairs, and into her bedroom. He frequently glances at the unconscious girl as if to determine what kind of person she might be. As they reach the threshold of her room, Belle is still wearing the drab clothing she had at home. While they pass to the other side, however, his magic graciously transforms her garments into a magnificent white gown worthy of a queen. When he places her on her bed, he stares at her face with a look that is sexual but also something more: it is an expression of focused admiration. From this, we know he will not harm or abuse her.

The whiteness of Belle's unblemished soul we have observed from her first appearance in the film. It does not alter much throughout the narrative, and some critics have assumed that she is a one-dimensional character who merely represents the ideal of vapid simplicity and submission to which young females have been traditionally subjected. It is sometimes claimed that she is not a real person but only a muse that might elicit male creativity and delight without having much earthy complexity in herself. But true as this may be to some extent, the whiteness of Cocteau's Belle is also a sign of her perfection as a creature who has a good heart befitting a storybook heroine who lives close to the goodness of nature.

In the scenes at home, Belle works in the fields and in the sunshine. After she has gone to the castle, her sisters, her brother, and Avenant are forced to do the outdoor chores that she once did. They cannot do them as well as she. When Belle returns from the castle in all her radiant finery, she utters with alarm: "Who has done my washing?" The whiteness of the linen we see is a reflection of herself, and Cocteau fills that sequence in the film with suggestive images of the large white sheets that are being hung out to dry. We are struck not only by the dazzling brightness of their coloration but also by the fact that this bit of labor in the open air has a visual / poetic beauty native to life in the country. It is an effect that Renoir would have relished.

The meaning of whiteness is also conveyed in the color of Magnifique, the horse who magically carries people to and from the castle. Cocteau's casting for the part ended only after he found just the white horse he had in mind. It was a professional who had been working in a circus, and therefore knew how to prance and even stride with great elegance and esprit. With his noble and high-stepping movements, Magnifique reveals that he has none of the dark bestiality of his master but rather is himself an offspring of Pegasus, or some other horse who soars above the earth. As we learn at the end, the Beast has a domain in those celestial regions, to which he transports Belle once he regains his princely power. Magnifique represents that capacity in him, his fellow beast before and after he has been liberated from the nefarious spell.

What emerges from this poetry of black and white is a dualism that thinkers have groped with for centuries. In modern thought Descartes' philosophy serves as a touchstone for the doctrine, but his careful arguments are also a codification and refinement of dualistic attitudes that long preceded him in French culture. In step with his twentieth-century repudiation of Cartesian premises, Cocteau tries to achieve, through his poetic effort, a harmonization between the two ontological categories. Just after the scene in which the Beast carries Belle into her room, she appears at dinner dressed in very splendid black attire. Without craving, as her sisters do, the material goods lavished upon her—the jewels, the banquet meals, the instant attendance of unseen but prescient servants—Belle has quickly accommodated herself to them. Though she finally rises into the heavens, she is being taken to some principality that also is a grandiose habitat somewhere on or near the earth. Unlike the dualism in Descartes and the Christian dogmas Descartes consciously reinforces, Cocteau's film is predicated upon a sense of ambivalent reconciliation between mind and matter, beauty and extreme ugliness, spiritual purity and plebeian delight in our carnal immersion once we accept the fact that it cannot be avoided.

The Cartesian dualism shows itself in the personality of the Beast. Cocteau presents him as a voracious predator whose nostrils quiver when his uncontrollable instincts detect the proximity of some animal to be killed and devoured. Returning from the hunt, he has lips and claws that drip with blood. Even before Belle's father meets the Beast, he sees on the ground in front of the castle the mutilated and bloodstained body of a deer. Belle, as well as her father, expect to be treated that way themselves. But in addressing the girl with great humility and showing subservience from the very beginning, the Beast resembles another type of animal, one that we all know well—a faithful dog or other domestic pet. As they do too, he combines the imperious and inhuman urgencies of nature with the sociable and uplifting capacity to rise above one's instincts. Since the same applies to people as well, the magic of Cocteau's myth accentuates his desire to reconcile the two elements in us as in other creatures, some of whom are worthy of being loved.

The Beast, who instantly falls in love with Belle and who resumes his human form once she expresses love for him, elicits our sympathy not only because of his good will toward the beautiful female he has captured but also because his intentions are respectable. He wants to marry Belle and make her his consort, instead of using her as a sexual object or plaything. One feels that Avenant's amorous eagerness is not the same, and that Belle rejects his overtures for that reason. Girls who love their father the way she does do get married, but only if they think their suitor will approximate the father's type of devotion and protectiveness.

In the last scene Belle reveals her problem to Prince Charming. Remarking that he looks like someone she knows, she confesses that she loved Avenant although she never told him so. In saying this, she seems somewhat abashed by her words, and the Prince lowers his eyes in disappointment. But when he asks whether she can love him although he only resembles that other person, she answers yes while also looking quizzically at him. Her hesitation can be taken as a bit of maidenly coyness or even coquettishness (as it is in the Disney movie). But more important, in Cocteau's film her response suggests the legitimate uncertainty she has toward this ornamental nobleman who has just thrust himself upon her. Grinning and dolled up as some kind of royalty, he is neither a flesh-and-blood male like Avenant nor a mysterious combination of kindliness and animal impulse like the Beast.

All three roles—Avenant, the Beast, and the Prince—are played by Jean Marais, adequately in the part of Avenant, superbly and with much insight as the Beast, but unconvincingly as a man trying to appear like a charming aristocrat. The questioning glance of Belle (beautifully enacted by Josette Day) reflects the fact that her growing and heartfelt love was directed toward the Beast rather than this mincing courtier in a glittering outfit who may not be really lovable and who may not be capable of loving her as she would like. When Greta Garbo saw Marais's transfiguration as the Prince in the film's first release, she whispered to a friend sitting next to her: "Give me back the Beast!"

Belle nevertheless accepts the challenge of this situation, as she has done with everything that preceded it. The Prince asserts that love can make an ugly man, himself as the Beast, into a handsome person. That is the official line, of course, and ingredient in Madame Leprince de Beaumont's attempt to get little girls to accept their parents' choice of a husband for them. But more telling is Belle's comment about the promised happiness she may possibly have by marrying the individual whose features resemble Avenant's while he himself presumably retains the Beast's ability to love. Her final words are "I'll have to get used to it." This expresses the pervasive ambivalence about life that Cocteau may likewise have felt, while also conveying an assurance—as in virtually all the myths of love—that through the imagination, at its best, a satisfying harmonization may occur as a human possibility.

Much has been written about the mythology of Beauty and her Beast in relation to the feelings that many people have toward the animals we eat but often revere as companions, in some cultures even worshiping them as aesthetic or religious beings. Underlying this bivalence, there is also the equivocal need we have for a love of *things* as well as a love of *persons*. Animals are often treated as things, but frequently as persons with whom we commune, converse, and share affective attachments. In the history of Western thought, which arrogates spiritual superiority to the human or superhuman as opposed to a beast's materiality, the prevailing doctrines deny that animals can be loved as persons. The experience of any normal child stands in refutation of such bigotry. But children have also been treated as inferior entities, on a par with animals themselves since both are regarded as deficient in the rationality that matters most. Usually written for the edification of children, but meaningful to adults as well, stories and myths about beauties who love beasts are designed to rectify and transcend these baleful assumptions.

In being the kind of enchanted animal that he is, the Beast appears as more than just a prince who has been made ugly by a wicked spell—as some children think that may have happened to themselves for some hidden reason. Within his natural order, the Beast suffers and seeks for love much as people do in every stage of life. At first Belle is horrified by his appearance because she considers him a wild and monstrous thing of the forest. When she (unknowingly) effects his salvation by accepting him as he is, she does so because she loves him in the way that she would love a human being who also needs her devotion. The total separation between loving animals or things and loving people as persons is thereby undermined.

As Hitchcock does when he fixates the camera on objects in the world—the key in Ingrid Bergman's fist, the razor in Gregory Peck's hand—Cocteau establishes his cinematic poetry by reference to things that are real like Hitchcock's but function within a world of magic. In *La Belle et la Bête*, they are not only the truncated hands and heads that are fascinating rather than disgusting, but also the mirror, the glove, the white horse, the key to Diana's pavilion, and the rose. The latter bears all the allegorical weight that adheres to this flower's resemblance to the female pudendum. At the same time, the magical "things" in Cocteau are always meaningful in their own context without being merely symbolic. Like the physical objects in the décor that serve by *not* being magical, they exemplify the overall ability of film "to show unreality with a realism that forces the spectator to believe in it."[8] That is why Cocteau claims that film exists as a genuine vehicle for poetry.

In a comparable vein he remarks that he chose the rural farmhouse that becomes a setting for his movie partly because of the small metal dragonhead that is affixed to an outside wall. In an exterior shot, Belle inadvertently touches this iron ring and its bizarre figurine. The Park of Raray outside Senlis was similarly useful. The sequence of the father looking for his horse on the morning after his night in the castle, and shouting for him from the top of a sculpted wall of large stone animals, was filmed in that locale.[9] The statues of dogs and other beasts, in a later scene even a huge stag, have their relevance as plausible inhabitants of the Beast's property. But also they remind us that the mere being of such creatures has been widely celebrated in all the arts. By lingering briefly on these sculptures in middle shots taken from below, Cocteau and his cinematographer Alekan augment the grandeur of Raray's monumental tribute to animality as a whole.

The vast allure in the myth that Cocteau updates resides in the fact that we know that we too are beasts: not only beasts but also persons who admire beauty and aspire to noble ideals that constitute (as Plato said) the spiritual dimension in our species. The pattern of this ambivalence and the other ones that I have mentioned is imaginatively presented in the myth of Cupid and Psyche as told by Apuleius in the first century AD. Psyche is renowned as the most beautiful woman in the world and sentenced for that by jealous Venus, who orders Cupid to sacrifice her to some ugly and fearful monster. Instead Cupid imprisons Psyche in a mountain cave where she is treated handsomely, and where he makes physical love to her on his nightly visits. Since Cupid is invisible, Psyche believes that her sexual lord does not want her to see how ugly he is. When she disobeys his commands by igniting a torch that reveals his identity as the winged and beautiful god of love, he flees. Her great travails then ensue, but eventually Cupid returns and marries her.

Leaving aside other ramifications in this story about the soul (Psyche) being admitted to the family of gods because of her beauty, and through a mutual bond of erotic love, what is most essential is the discovery that a nocturnal visitor for sexual purposes may not be bestial but also possibly divine. The ending is a joyous one since it overcomes our sense of malaise in being both body and spirit.

Variations upon this theme occur in films like *Dr. Jekyll and Mr. Hyde*, *The Phantom of the Opera*, *King Kong*, *Frankenstein*, *The Hunchback of Notre Dame*, and many others—in all of which monsters love a beautiful woman and seek to be transformed by her beauty, in addition to whatever capability for love she may have, into something more ideal. A highly sophisticated version of the myth is embodied in Oscar Wilde's *The Picture of Dorian Gray*. It has been the basis of at least two films and is perfectly suited to the cinematic depiction of the split between increasing moral decay, recorded in Dorian's portrait, and the unchanging beauty of his physical appearance.

In this variation, as in the ones I listed, the conclusion is not at all a happy one. Sibyl Vane's love for Dorian leads to her death; Dorian murders the artist who lovingly paints the picture of his beautiful face; and when he himself slashes the painting, he is turned into his own horrid reality. The protagonist's name conveys the unresolved antithesis between body and spirit that Wilde expresses in all his writings. *Dorian* suggests Greek exemplars of beauty while *Gray* implies an ominous though perhaps very elegant region between black and white. In this narrative no one's love can harmonize the alternatives; and despite Dorian's good looks, both in life and in the picture at first, we surmise that moral turpitude exists in him from the start, though entirely revealed only later in the aesthetic truthfulness of the painting. His attractive veneer is thus an illusion that he and others have fabricated as a way of hiding what he is in fact. The ugliness of his deeds registers nonetheless in the progressively altered features that the camera shows us throughout his decline, and then in its totality in the uncanny picture. No novel could likely emulate this combination of visual effects.

In its sheer cinematography, Cocteau's *La Belle et la Bête* is, in my opinion, one of the most beautiful films in the history of cinema. It is a type of beauty coherent with his attempt to present the unreality of magic and enchantment as another world that exists within our own reality and not as merely an imposed phantasmagoria of the one we normally experience. Though Cocteau likens this inner reality to the nature of a dream, as we have seen, he wishes to give an accurate account of the unreality in a dream. At the same time, his movie sometimes contains realistic elements that are clearly dreamlike. For instance, when Belle enters the castle for the first time and passes through a long hallway lined with windows and billowing drapes, she does not walk. As an expression of her amazement, she floats toward the camera. In the studio she was standing on a gliding platform that gently moved her across the floor. That is not only a masterful trick, but also true to the feeling one often gets in dreams. For the most part, however, the reality of the unreal is presented as comparable to our daily and daytime reality in life without the idiosyncratic dreaminess of a dream.

To attain this end, Cocteau hardly ever uses special effects. An exception occurs when Belle gives her jeweled necklace to one of her sisters and it turns into a twisted rope on the ground. But this too occurs in the rural, outdoor context of the white sheets being hung out to dry. For the interiors of the farmhouse, Cocteau chose a design that is reminiscent of realistic paintings by Vermeer as well as Rembrandt's *Anatomy Lesson*. For the father's trip through the stormy forest, he copied Gustave Doré's famous illustrations in the fairytales of Perrault that make them seem to be quaint and simplified portrayals of ordinary life considered appropriate for childhood mentality. To attain the realism of his enchanted castle, Cocteau provided not only the living statues and recognizable though magical appurtenances of a luxurious habitat but also natural growths—flowers, vines, small trees that spread across Belle's bedroom and shed their scattered leaves or branches on the stone steps outside the building.

By interpenetrating the real and the unreal in this manner, Cocteau enables the grown-ups in his audience to which the film is directed to make the suspension of disbelief that comes so easily to those who are very young. In a handwritten note at the beginning of the film, he implores his spectators to revert to the imaginativeness of children in order to savor the artistic qualities of the make-believe that he creates as a poet. The opening credits appear in chalk on a blackboard and are hastily scribbled in his own hand, as if he were a teacher in a schoolroom. But, having placed these ideas in the consciousness of his adult viewers, he then has the actors (dressed in civilian clothes) erase their own names in a gesture that the camera speeds up each time as an assertion in its peculiar way that this medium is not limited to pedestrian reality. That is reinforced when a technician intervenes with a clapboard that has the words *Cocteau* and *Alekan* on it. The film itself then follows.

Cocteau's maneuvers in this regard are comparable to those of Laurence Olivier in *Henry V*, which was released a few years earlier. In order to help the viewer adjust to the artificiality of real people being presented as speaking in the poetic language of Shakespeare's play, Olivier used backdrops that were obviously unreal, though appropriate to the medieval period in which the historical events take place. The backdrops were drawn from the miniatures known as *Les Très Riches Heures du Duc de Berri*. Though these works are as artificial as the poetry of Shakespeare, they are relics of the particular moment in time during which the narrative unfolds. In that sense the reality of the unreal furthers the unreality of imagination, which is a real component of human nature that permeates this (like any other) artistic effort. In the case of *Henry V*, the device also alerts us to the fact that imagination's ideological constructions in the Middle Ages may themselves have contributed to the motivation of the historical persons that Shakespeare portrays.

Fertile though Olivier's "bright idea," as he calls it, surely was, it seems like a primitive forerunner of what Cocteau achieves. Extending Olivier's minor effect to enclose the magic of filmmaking itself, Cocteau applies it to mythic storytelling in general, and specifically in examples of magic and enchantment that arise from a mode of imagination that projects the ontological being of mythology. Neither Olivier nor Shakespeare and his source in Holinshed conceived of these ramifications.

Cocteau also amplifies something Olivier said about the presentation of Shakespearean verse. In a televised interview,

Olivier remarked that both in film and onstage an actor must learn how to unite the realism and the poetry in Shakespeare, the first of which requires a prosaic mode of delivery quite different from the musicality of the latter. Despairing of his inability to make the notion precise, Olivier concludes: "You have to find the truth *through* the verse. Now if that's understandable, then that's the only answer I can give you."[10]

As if in contradiction to this idea, or rather as a means of amplifying it, every aspect of Cocteau's film—including the commonplace country scenes—augments the cinematic poetry. In all three of his roles, Marais speaks his lines in the sonorous manner of someone performing Corneille or Racine at the Comédie-Française. Far from seeming stilted or archaic, this type of talking gives the utterances of Avenant, Prince Charming, and especially the Beast an aura of numinous import that only poetry can convey. It is the same combination of real and unreal that Olivier uses at the beginning of *Henry V*, when the all-too-human actor becomes a regal person in the fiction once he steps on stage, but later returns to his quotidian appearance after the curtain comes down and he takes his bows. At that time we see that Katharine, too, is not what she seemed but only a boy dressed like a princess. Still Cocteau does something more. By joining the magic in the film with the cinematic magic of mythmaking, he creates an aesthetic artifact that replicates the amorphous character of human reality as a whole.

In a similar effort Cocteau borrows a gimmick that he learned from Orson Welles's *Citizen Kane*. Just as Welles often leaves in obscurity the borders of corridors and other spatial areas in order to enlarge them in the spectator's perception, Cocteau treats the entire interior of the castle in that fashion. It's a trick of the camera that sustains Belle's floating feeling of unlimited wonder. But for Cocteau all this belongs to a story that—unlike Welles's—elicits the fluid sensibility that the making of myths creates generically.[11] Welles tells us that he wanted to *examine* myths rather than be a mythmaker himself as John Ford was. Cocteau is like Ford in this regard, and not like Welles.

As in Cocteau's other films, the mythology in his version of *Beauty and the Beast* explores the relation between life and death, above all their transition into each other. The fable of Madame Leprince de Beaumont sought to assure young girls that their virtue can purify the beastliness of a future husband and even turn him into a charming princeling who will transport his wife to a land of matrimonial joy. In revising this perspective, Cocteau addresses the more plausible situation of the carnal but well-intentioned male in search of a good-hearted female.

Some commentators have even thought of his film as a movie seen from the man's point of view, and at least one calls attention to Cocteau's homoerotic fixation upon the face of his intimate friend Marais.[12] While both of these interpretations are valid to some extent, they are also shortsighted. The various close-ups that are given to Marais make prominent his importance in a story about a monster who ends up looking like Avenant's double while Avenant becomes the monster himself. In this complex transaction, life and death interpenetrate, as they do in all the vegetative and animal processes of nature, and in the inscrutable mysteries by which we perpetuate the qualities of our biological forebears. That is what the film is about. The sexual love that may or may not have guided the filmmaker's imagination is surely a lesser consideration.

While counterbalancing the original emphasis upon the problems of nubile females with a matching concern about the masculinity of the Beast, Cocteau does not neglect the basic purity of Belle and her devotion to an aging and suddenly impoverished father. She delays marrying Avenant because she fears her father might die without her. It is not insignificant that, in winning her hand, Prince Charming says the father will live with them in his kingdom in the sky. A post-Freudian interpretation of the myth, such as Bruno Bettelheim's, does not properly elucidate this equilibration between life and death from the female's point of view no less than the male's. In *The Uses of Enchantment*, Bettelheim elaborates the oedipal relationship between the father and his daughter Belle. He reads the tale as a depiction of how "the oedipal love of Beauty for her father, when transferred to her future husband, is wonderfully healing" for all three of them.[13] Of greater significance, however, is the degree to which Belle assumes the maternal role in the dysfunctional family that Cocteau studies in this as in other dramatic and cinematic works of his.

Belle rises to the occasion not as a child who fantasizes the displacement of her mother but rather as a mature person who acts heroically for the benefit of her worthless siblings as well as her father. As her reward she acquires a superlative mate whom she has freed from an imprisonment more devastating than the restraint he had imposed upon her when he was the Beast. She behaves much as Leonora does in liberating Florestan in Beethoven's *Fidelio*.

Far from being a "man's movie," Cocteau's film can be seen as preeminently a woman's movie on a par with the Beethoven opera. But while the latter celebrates the optimistic prospect of universal freedom for all men and women, Cocteau's heroine aspires to a more humble, more plausible, goal that is less difficult to achieve. It is also more realistic and more personal: the first inasmuch as it recognizes the inseparability of life and death; the second because Cocteau is expressing his intuitive view of his own life and death as a poet. I will return to this theme later in the chapter, but here I want to reexamine Cocteau's first film. As its title informs us, it deals with the *blood* of a poet. One can think of that as the vitality—the lifeblood—that infuses whatever is truly artistic as well as being organic fluid drained in the course of creativity by the self-sacrificial suffering to which poets like Cocteau must submit.

In *La Belle et la Bête*, the blood we see on the lips and claws of the Beast, and on the deer he has killed, represent the inevitability of death as a constant component of life. Having grown up on a farm, Belle understands this fact of nature. Though she is revolted by the hunting instinct that enslaves the Beast, she does not seek to reform him. After her admission that she loves a man (Avenant) who loves her, the Beast rushes wildly into the forest and then returns from an orgy of killing in a dazed condition and dripping with blood. Belle berates him for entering her chamber in such a state, but that is all she says.

Previously, while they are talking out-of-doors, his ears quiver when he has suddenly sniffed prey nearby and compulsive forces put him into a kind of predatory stupor. Belle scolds him for being inattentive to her remarks but not because he is reacting like a beast. As if she were a schoolmarm or insulted consort, she says "Where *are* you?" and "I am talking to you!" Death and slaughter being engrained in the animal condition, she seeks merely to socialize and civilize what is beastlike in us all. That is a role wives have often performed in marriage. Once the Beast and Avenant have lost their lives, in different ways,

Belle surmounts the hazard of mortality, the losing of the blood of life, which preoccupied Cocteau throughout his existence as a poet.

Though it differs from *Fidelio* in this respect, Cocteau's version of the fable is amenable to a similar kind of operatic rendition. Serving a comparable mythology of female heroism and attainment, in this case premarital rather than postmarital, it also resembles *Fidelio* in having sequences at the beginning that provide an opéra comique introduction to the more serious music and dramatic development that will follow. The background score that Georges Auric wrote for the soundtrack usually adds little to the early scenes in the farmhouse. Apart from suggestions of French bergamasque melodies of the seventeenth century during the opening credits, Auric wisely holds back his main contribution until the father's trip into the forest. The music then, and at later moments in the castle, is adventuresome and awe-inspired. While the father passes through the corridor of hands holding candlesticks, his astonishment is intensified by orchestral silence; but his departure is accompanied by a celestial choir that increases the wonderment of this place.

When Belle makes her own entrance there, the music is gently affirmative as she encounters one marvel after another. The musical support ends only after the Beast suddenly arrives to prevent her escape and she faints away. Thereafter Auric's score varies from discreet enhancement in scenes that have dramatic dialogue to brilliant and insightful explication of what is being felt or done in sequences without language in them. When Belle mounts Magnifique in order to sacrifice herself out of love for her father, and later to return to the castle because the dying Beast needs her, the music highlights the heroic parameters of her courageous character. Much of the beauty in this film results from the sonic effects that Auric provided.

Philip Glass's operatic version of Cocteau's work is totally different. It is an innovative experiment in what Glass calls "opera / film." In it the composer retains all the visual properties of the 1946 movie but none of its sound. Glass changes the Cocteau movie in two ways. Having completely eliminated the spoken language, he dubs in voices of the various characters, who sing his lyrical version of what they say in the original production; and also he inserts background music of his own in substitution for Auric's. The result is only partly successful. Glass's harmonies are sometimes very beguiling but often intrusive. Since he was writing sung rather than spoken exchanges between all the characters, his musical presence runs throughout the film instead of being selective, or very meaningful in its selectivity, as Auric's always is. Moreover, the music of Glass is not only uniform—even repetitious—for long stretches but also frequently constrained to a simulation of a dreamlike condition. Given Cocteau's steadfast effort to portray the reality of the unreal as opposed to a nebulous representation of it, one is struck by the degree to which Glass deviates from the goals of the movie he is making into an opera, derived from it but not truly based on it.

This is not to say that the composer of any opera has to remain faithful to a literary or cinematic source that has inspired him. But in this case, the changes are especially troubling because they reappear in the gross misinterpretation of Cocteau's poetic intention that occurs in Glass's prose introduction to his opera. These comments accompany the performance of his work in the Criterion Collection DVD of *La Belle et la Bête* (2003). Glass there maintains that for Cocteau: "The rose represents beauty, the aesthetic object of the work. The horse represents strength and determination. The key, technique and control of materials. The mirror, the path. And finally the glove represents nobility—the confidence and ease with which the artist enters his vocation."[14] I have no reason to doubt the authenticity of Glass's claim that these are preconceptions that an artist *might* entertain. But in fact they signify a symbolization of reality—not just a portrayal of it—that is entirely foreign to the aesthetics that Cocteau himself espoused and consistently employed in his mythological films, above all in his Orphic Triad but also in *La Belle et la Bête*.

Though Cocteau's *Orphée* may not be as beautiful a film as *La Belle et la Bête*, it is often thought to be his supreme achievement in filmmaking. Aside from his inventiveness as a metteur en scène, which I will discuss, his mastery of the art form in *Orphée* (1949) derives from his imaginative variations upon strands of Western mythology that he intertwines throughout that film as well as its sequel *The Testament of Orpheus* (1959). The theme of a person traveling to the underworld, Hades, in the hope of releasing a beloved husband from the clutch of death occurs in the Greek myth of Alcestis. She is a devoted woman, however, and therefore not an artist of any sort that women could later become. Orpheus is depicted in Ovid and other sources as a poet-musician whose talent entrances the gods of the netherworld and elicits their compassion. In Cocteau's reconstruction of the myth, Orpheus's condition as both a loving spouse and a man supremely dedicated to his art becomes the basis of a cinematic exploration of fundamental ambiguities in human nature, above all in creative persons.

Orphée's violent outbursts and frequent insensitivity perturb his wife Eurydice, but she constantly expresses her belief that they have a perfect marriage. Heurtebise, the somewhat fallen angel in this version of the myth, is a peripheral male in their marriage, a friend who loves Eurydice without being her lover. Having lost his prior mortality, he can no longer experience the sexual feelings that any pair of spouses might crave. Nevertheless, or possibly because of this, he perceives the imperfections in Orphée's treatment of Eurydice, who is unable to comprehend them. Heurtebise represents us in the audience as sympathetic observers of the marital difficulties of the great poet and his faithful wife.

As they are with ordinary people, these difficulties are occasioned by the man's adulterous attitude toward some other female. In *Orphée* she is La Princesse, but also more than human. Just as Orphée is a wonder-working artist, so too is she a woman who once lived on earth but has now become Death in one of its manifestations. Heurtebise is her subordinate. In descending to the "zone," the intermediary region of those who are no longer alive, Orphée travels in pursuit of La Princesse / Death as well as the wife he wishes to retrieve. In Cocteau's Orphic Triad, which begins with *The Blood of a Poet* and ends with *The Testament of Orpheus*, the artist's quest for death that signifies his special mission in life is always foremost.

The theme of a social hero or other exceptional individual fulfilling his destiny by seeking death in conjunction with the life-enhancing love of a woman who is devoted to him recurs throughout Western mythology in various forms. The Flying Dutchman, as in Richard Wagner's early opera, circles the globe in his own zone of misery until an exceptional woman recognizes his heroic status, loves him, and is even willing to die for him. At that point they find in death a consummatory merging they both desire. In *The Ring of the Niebelungen,* Brünnhilde is cast into her deathlike slumber because she acted out of romantic love for Sigmund and thereby defied the orders of her father Wotan. In *Orphée* the character Death repudiates the powers that be by sacrificing herself in order to help the poet transcend his human limitations and attain the immortality of creative genius.

As she had foreseen, she and Heurtebise are then condemned to some unspeakable punishment whose nature is finally disclosed in *The Testament of Orpheus*. It consists in being forced to serve as a judge (for which one might also read, a critic) of what others do or feel. Death and Heurtebise have both been found guilty of the sin of loving a mortal—Orphée in her case, Eurydice in the case of Heurtebise.

In film mythologizing, death frequently appears under the guise of resembling, or actually being, a man or woman. In Wim Wenders's *Wings of Desire,* there is a multitude of invisible "messengers" who conduct the dead to their final destination. These angels of death are benign, as they are usually portrayed in recent movies. In Wenders's film, and in its American remake, *City of Angels,* one of the messengers falls in love with a woman who then reciprocates his love. To unite with her and feel what lovers do, he must forfeit his immortality. He makes that sacrifice and joyously experiences the feelings and desires that mortals have. An ending of this sort is a happy one and quite coherent with the basic design of Romantic ideology. Cocteau's approach moves in an alternate direction.

Presenting the outcome of the poet's profound love for Death and her sacrifice on his behalf, Cocteau does arrange for Orphée to return to life and renew his marital attachment—now elevated to an even higher level than before. He succeeds in bringing Eurydice back to her place within their felicitous and even burgeoning family. This deviates from the Greek and Roman versions, which culminate in the defeat of Orpheus's venture and his subsequent death at the hands of vengeful women. Toward the conclusion of *Orphée*, we see him cheerfully ensconced in the warmth of his homespun marriage, the former adventure seeming to him like a strange dream. A precedent for this benign outcome existed in the denouement of Gluck's eighteenth-century opera *Orphée et Eurydice*, where Amour descends as a deus ex machina to reunite the married couple on earth. But the final scene of Cocteau's movie is given to Death, who must face her fate in the zone. Her eyes fill with tears as she remembers her devastating loss and foresees her punishment. In its portrayal of that grim reality, this ending is anything but happy.

By establishing his reigning ambiguity, Cocteau reinforces its underlying message about the uncertain or pluralistic, and even absurd, character of human nature. As the years went by, however, he must have regretted his affirmative rendition of what had originally led to a pessimistic outcome for the two spouses. In *The Testament of Orpheus*, he informs us that the second revival of Eurydice and the marital bliss that ensues for her and Orphée was just a brief interlude that could not alter the deeper forces in existence: "On ne peut pas cracher dans le vent" (One cannot spit into the wind). Eurydice must therefore die definitively, and Orpheus cannot escape his fate as a lonely artist whom lesser mortals will maliciously destroy.

That trenchant view about the human confrontation with death runs parallel to the last act of Thornton Wilder's play *Our Town*. Having died in childbirth, Emily joins the other deceased townspeople in their solemn community in the cemetery on the hill. When she says she would like to revisit the land of the living, the others advise her not to do so. It will only sadden her, they insist. She bravely makes the attempt, coming back to life at a memorable moment in the past—her twelfth birthday. Standing in the kitchen of her family's house as a ghost who is not seen or heard by those who were then alive but also present as herself on that occasion, she is crushed by what she sees. In its rapidity for all of us, time itself, she now realizes, keeps us from fully experiencing our temporal duration. "It goes so fast. We don't have time to look at one another. . . . So all that was going on and we never noticed. Take me back . . . to my grave."[15]

In its exquisite fidelity to sentiments about death and the nature of lived time that every sensitive human being must surely have felt, this final sequence in the play is one of the great pinnacles of theatrical art. When it reappeared in the Hollywood version of *Our Town* (1940), the forceful impact of the scene was completely eroded. As we learn at the finale, Emily's revelation occurs within a fitful dream that she has had while giving birth to her beautiful baby. We are elated by the sight of her holding it in her arms, surrounded by her smiling husband and all the goodness of their joyous family.

Duplicating this approach at a time when France was still reeling from the shame and hardship of World War II, Cocteau might have felt that *Orphée*, like *Our Town* in its American film production, had to have an optimistic conclusion. In *The Testament of Orpheus*, thirteen years later, Cocteau's revised attitude shows itself in the first scene, prefatory to the rest of the movie. He repeats the footage of *Orphée* that showed a close-up of Death's face as hot and copious tears stream down it in a demonstration of her pain. Later on, when Cocteau delivers the lines about the ultimate death of Eurydice and then Orphée, he seems intent upon portraying himself as a moribund poet, though still active in his art. That may have made the difference in his interpretation of the myth.

The attempt to combine positive and negative approaches to death is very common in the history of film. As one highly imaginative exemplar, we should consider, once again, Ingmar Bergman's *The Seventh Seal*. In it Death appears as a man rather than a woman. His face is painted white, which itself suggests a relevant ambiguity. The facial decoration of the actors as they perform on stage is also white. And though Death is attired in black throughout and is unrelenting in his black-hearted search for chosen victims, he has an amusing penchant for playing chess. He is willing to spare the Knight as long as their game continues, or if the Knight wins the match. Romantic love has often been likened to a game of chess between a man and a woman. The Knight is clearly an embattled male, and Death's white makeup suggests his resemblance to an astute female who is being playful with the prey she will eventually demolish.

In this match both participants cheat, as lovers often do. By pretending to be a priest, Death takes advantage of the Knight's description, in confession, of his chessboard strategy. Then, in the forest, the Knight sweeps the pieces off the board, as if by accident but really to help the holy family escape. Except for the fact that Jof, Mia, and the baby do live on in their supreme love for each other, there is no happy outcome in *The Seventh Seal*. Even so, the beguiling humanity of Death provides an affirmative subtext to the grim struggle with personal annihilation that everyone has to endure merely in being alive.

Moreover, the ability of the Knight to perform his heroic service as a protector of the faith expresses an idealistic and uplifting approach to life that outweighs the cynical disbelief that the world-weary squire Jöns voices time and again. But while the squire makes no progress in his pilgrim's passage, and scarcely recognizes the meaningfulness of his own good deeds in comforting the pitiful witch and defending Jof as well as the mute girl from the evil of a corrupted representative of the church, the Knight fulfills his mission in life. His alienated wife validates that by finally accepting him back. And as a sanctified chorus to his passionate praying to a divinity whose existence the squire continues to deny, the mute girl has the last word when she repeats Christ's utterance on the cross: "It is finished."

If we ask ourselves how the word *it* is to be understood in this context, we would be mistaken to think Bergman meant only that his story ends at that point. As in the gospels, what is finished is the uniquely preordained mission of a spiritual hero, whose task has finally been completed. The Knight's appreciation of the ideal significance of his mythic role on earth had been renewed in him during the scene in which he takes a meal with the holy family. Mia serves him milk and wild strawberries as they and the others sit on a hillside under a clear sky, enjoying the summer's twilight evening. Jof plays with the baby who will someday master the impossible trick of keeping a juggler's ball aloft indefinitely. The Knight has returned from the Crusades wearied by the futility of disastrous warfare. Though a casual member of the group, his faith in the potential sanctity of life is now replenished.

As in relation to Cocteau's films, we in the audience can also experience the validity of this poetic proclamation about aesthetic features in our existence. As if to confess that he too is unable to fathom either the metaphysical uncertainties of his efforts or even his ability to transmute them into a work of art, Bergman intimates that he himself is "the fool" who is being dragged by Death along with everyone else in the penultimate moments of the movie. The image of Death and his roped captives is filmed at so great a distance that we cannot see the face of that individual, whoever he or she may be, possibly Skat the actor and stage director but possibly not. I imagine him or her as a surrogate for the filmmaker. Jof observes the horrifying spectacle in one of his "visions." Though he is a man of acute and active imagination, as Ingmar Bergman was, he has also called himself a fool and may now be using that word to identify the fellow visionary artist who created him.[16]

Despite his kinship with Bergman, Cocteau in both *Orphée* and *The Testament of Orpheus* treats the character of Death differently, and within a variant mythology. Bergman was trying to make sense of the severe Protestant faith into which he was born. In the matter of affirmation or rejection of it, he argues for each side in turn and leaves us to decide about our own commitment to one or the other. Cocteau writes and directs from a postmodernist point of view in which literal truth or falsity is no longer a burning issue. In *The Seventh Seal* Bergman observes medieval and later Christianity from his contemporary stance of indecision. Cocteau affirms the ambiguity and absurdity of life itself as a fundamental doctrine to which he strongly subscribes.

In making Death a woman who loves Orphée as he loves her, in other words romantically and with libidinal desire, Cocteau unites two types of myth—one about death and the other about interpersonal attachment among human beings. Announcing herself to Orphée, Death says that she is *his* death. She uses the same words in her relation to Cégeste; but he is a lesser poet, not a master of the art comparable to Orphée. In proclaiming her special bonding with the latter, Death employs the slogan of absolute merging that lovers use in the Romantic tradition that Cocteau presupposes.

L'Eternel retour (*The Eternal Return*), which was directed by Jean Delannoy but written and supervised by Cocteau, is a retelling of the myth of Tristan and Iseult in a version that incorporates Cocteau's film aesthetics as well as his ideas about love and death. On an introductory card, he informs us that he has borrowed Nietzsche's concept of eternal recurrence and that it applies to the reappearance of great myths of mankind throughout the ages. That interpretation is wildly inaccurate. Nietzsche was trying to formulate a theory about the nature of reality and not about the less momentous fact that some myths continue endlessly in their varied formulations.

For our immediate purposes, we need only note that *L'Eternel retour* renews Cocteau's attempt to present realistically narrative elements that are magical and unreal. Many embodiments of the Tristan myth in the last eight hundred years have expunged the poisonous love potion that leads to the suffering of the lovers. The possibility that any such thing can even exist was vigorously denied by Gottfried von Strassburg, whose naturalistic novel in the fourteenth century remains as one of the greatest enactments of this myth in all its permutations.

In Cocteau's adaptation we are left with an unresolvable ambiguity about the so-called love potion. On the one hand, a passionate explosion of love occurs immediately after the

Tristan and Iseult characters (Patrice and Natalie) partake of it. Natalie had previously remarked that she does not believe in magic, and Patrice says something comparable after the fateful event. All the same, Cocteau's script avails itself of common accoutrements of enchantment. The drinking of the potion occurs in the midst of a violent storm that accentuates—with loud thunderbolts and the blinding effect of tempestuous lightning—the extraordinary nature of what is happening. On the other hand, the man and woman have been drinking alcohol in order to induce a drunken state in themselves; they have previously made incipient gestures of erotic affiliation; and they are jointly suffering through the boredom of living in the same chateau as Mark, whom Natalie does not love, and his obnoxious relatives, whom Patrice cannot abide.

All this is depicted realistically, and even the suggestion of a magical aphrodisiac may be taken as a bit of poetic metaphor that can be allowed in even a twentieth-century realist. Nevertheless, the ambiguity remains. As Hamlet says to Horatio: "There are more things in heaven and earth than are dreamt of in your philosophy." To which Cocteau might reply: "But, of course, Shakespeare does not tell us what they are. No one can."

Death has its place in Cocteau's film about Tristan and Iseult, but not because the lovers are "really" in love with it. That is how Denis de Rougement interprets the meaning in every version of the myth. Though this reading may possibly apply to Cocteau's Orphic Triad, *L'Eternel retour* resists any such approach. The sickness unto death that Natalie and Patrice undergo comes from the defeat of their search for life-enriching love rather than a desire to leave the land of the living. Natalie recounts the gloominess of her former existence, but she is not suicidal.

When Mark forgives her in the snow-filled mountain scene, she accepts his domination and returns to her earlier condition of submissiveness. Her health declines as a result, and when she lays herself down and dies next to the dead Patrice, we know that this world cannot accommodate the wholesome value of their love for each other.

Congruent with the perspective that I have been discussing, Cocteau's ending of the film is a morphic transformation of the locale in which the lovers have died. That took place in a fisherman's shack that houses a rowboat turned upside down, upon which Patrice and then Natalie expire. In the final shot, the shack magically becomes a bare chapel with arcades that open upon a clarified background. In it the two lovers lie side by side on blocks of stone suggestive of parallel altars. Having been tense and laden with anguish in the previous scene, the music is now supportive and uplifted. In some of the medieval sources, the local peasantry bury the couple at opposite ends of a chapel. From Tristan's plot of land there grows a vine of honeysuckle that reaches over to, and entangles with, a rose that rises from Iseult's burial ground. The peasants cut down these plants three times, but the fourth time they desist. The number three may be interpreted as a Trinitarian symbol, and the fourth as nature joined with divinity in a fulfillment that completes the mystery of human life. Cocteau's culminating image does not extend that far, but it conveys a sense of positive and affirmative closure to the sufferings of these lovers.

In *The Testament of Orpheus*, when Cocteau says that the happiness of Orphée and Eurydice at the end of the prequel was only a slight interlude before death whisks them both away, he seems to be now repudiating any overly optimistic elements in his unwavering ambiguities about love. And indeed he incorporates in the later film images of Iseult on a sailboat at sea looking endlessly for her Tristan, but never finding him or achieving anything like the quasi-religious resolution built into the version I have just described. He also shows blinded Oedipus weeping in his misery as he staggers aimlessly and without the spiritual catharsis that Sophocles emphasizes. In another scene Cocteau parodistically repeats the agony of K in Kafka's *The Trial* as he is subjected to one bureaucratic lie after another while hoping to be admitted to the center of ultimate power—in this case, the goddess Minerva. And once he has reached her and offered her the magic flower he has brought as a gift, she kills him.

In a trick effect we have seen before, Cocteau springs back to life, suddenly erect and apparently unaltered by his demise. To his companion Cégeste he explains that this is only one of the many deaths that he has had to experience in his life as a poet. The idea of creativity entailing a multitude of deaths that the artist learns how to survive may derive from Proust or even Gide, but in his cinematic aesthetic Cocteau puts it to excellent use on his own. It introduces an advanced outlook that *The Blood of a Poet* does not have. That work, rightly considered as a preliminary in Cocteau's Orphic Triad, expresses the poet's self-pitying feeling that society and the world, which are themselves crumbling like the smokestack, mercilessly ignore the recurrent deaths a sensitive and creative person must undergo simply because he is unlike, and better than, anyone else. At a time in his life when he knows that his own extinction is not far off, Cocteau seems to have reached a stage of acceptance of his fatality that he never had before.

This acceptance, and vibrant self-affirmation, vividly appears in *The Testament of Orpheus* after Cocteau has been harpooned by Minerva and before he comes back to life. Having been carried to a kind of sarcophagus by his admirers and by the Flamenco-singing gypsies whose defiantly artistic lifestyle he admires, his body oozes blood from its wound. We see it as a crimson insert into the movie, all the rest of which is black-and-white. This is the blood of the poet in its fullest coloration and most life-assertive manifestation, like the blood of Christ. Self-pity has finally been eliminated from the self-referential myth.

Two other films of Cocteau are worth mentioning, both based on plays of his and both dealing with his characteristic views about love and death. They have matching titles: *Les Enfants terribles*, narrated by the voice of Cocteau though directed by Jean-Pierre Melville, and *Les Parents terribles*. Each ends with the melodramatic and suicidal death of the female protagonist. In the first, she is the all-but-incestuous sister of a poetic teenage brother whose love for another girl elicits the dysfunctional hatred that mars the relationship between the siblings. The "other woman" in this triangle has facial features described as remarkably similar to those of a charismatic chum of the young fellow. The homosexual and autobiographical implications of that had already been presented in *The Blood of a Poet*, in which the chum also appears. In this movie, the brother takes poison at the end and the sister shoots herself with ferocious determination that implies a love of death. In her final speech she denies being insane and insists that those who seek the interpersonal love she has now wrecked are the deranged ones.

In *Les Parents terribles* the self-destructive woman is the mother of a son in his twenties who falls in love with a beautiful woman who has been the mistress of his father. At first none of them knows that the lovers are related to each other—a variation on the Tristan motif in which Iseult sleeps with both King Mark and his nephew. When that circumstance is brought to light and love between the young couple seems to be on its way to becoming triumphant, the pathological mother kills herself. Though she has never loved her husband, she feels thwarted by his having loved the other woman. The greatest loss for her, however, is living without the selfish and possessive oneness she formerly shared with her devoted son. His normal sexual love has shattered all vestiges of that in her imagination. Dying as she does, she allows death to cast its shadow over any possible marital happiness he and his wife might now experience.

Asked about Cocteau's films, Bergman replied: "I consider *Orphée* one of the most beautiful French films ever made. . . . I liked less *Beauty and the Beast*, which seemed to me too contrived."[17] We can hardly surmise what he thought of Cocteau's *Terribles* movies.

Since Cocteau viewed his cinematic efforts as visual poetry, and since he repudiated the merely "poetic" as false to the materiality of our existence, his mythmaking systematically employs physical entities that are common in our reality. I have already listed the five most prominent ones in *La Belle et la Bête*: the mirror, the glove, the white horse Magnifique, the rose (which is also white), and the key to Diana's pavilion. These articles of daily life reappear in the other films, but are always molded to fit the different twists and turns of each narrative.

In *La Belle et la Bête* the mirror has two properties that are conventional in fairy tales. As we might expect, it yields a visual image of some person or event that is not actually present at the moment. It is a kind of television. But even apart from that modern invention, any audience that has grown up with make-believe would automatically recognize this remarkable potentiality of mirrors. We find nothing odd in Belle's ability to call up images of her father or the Beast by looking into her hand mirror or the one in her magic bedroom. As a poet, Cocteau knows how to help us enjoy the prospect of extending our visual field, and thereby appreciate its actuality more fully than we might have otherwise. The first time we see Belle she is scrubbing the floor in her father's house. Being a perfectionist, she makes it as clean and pellucid as a mirror even though a floor is something we walk on and usually do not look into. To achieve the metaphoric effect he has in mind, Cocteau positions the camera at an angle that shows us Belle's image clearly reflected in the floor she is washing. Avenant even comments on that.

Other properties of Cocteau's magical mirrors are intriguing. Through cognitive powers of their own, they can sometimes reveal hidden truths. When the nasty sisters look into Belle's mirror, they do not perceive someone at a distance but rather themselves as they really are. One of them sees herself as an old and grotesquely ugly woman; the other sees a monkey that we interpret as a simian representation of her subhuman qualities. Throughout the Orphic Triad mirrors also serve as the means by which a poet can escape our mortal coil and enter into the more fundamental being that Death inhabits and that she travels to and from effortlessly. In *The Blood of a Poet*, the poet has great difficulty with this feat until the statue to whom he has unknowingly given life encourages him to keep on trying.

He finally succeeds by throwing himself into the mirror with a splash that implies that it requires a total giving of oneself, a release of mind and body similar to diving into a pool.

Though Orphée is presented as a superlative poet, he fails completely in his attempt to follow Death and Heurtebise through the mirror until the latter teaches him the secret of its technology. You have to put on the gloves that Death employed while practicing her mystic rites. Then with gloved hands joined as if in prayer, you point them into the mirror and thus penetrate its seeming hardness. Being revelatory of transcendent truths, mirrors in *Orphée* naturally break when confronted with some falsity or sign of ignorance, as the one in La Princesse's living room does because Orphée cannot understand who she might be. Once he learns the truth about her, he uses the gloves and walks through mirrors as artfully as Death and Heurtebise.

Communication with some outer reality also occurs by means of the radio messages that Orphée hears first in the house of the Princesse and later in the car she leaves in his garage. On an auditory level, they resemble the uncanny effect of mirror images. The sounds come from nowhere on earth that we can readily recognize, but they provide an important service. They seem like bits of nonsense, until Orphée transcribes them into lines of poetry that are often beautiful and that a group of aesthetes in one scene consider some of his best work. While Cocteau is obviously poking fun at these feckless (though dangerous) critics, the idea that poetry is a kind of sonic and verbal discourse whose import exceeds ordinary modes of meaning is basic in his thinking. The hidden realism of this aural communication also registers in the fact that audiences in 1950 would certainly identify such coded messages with the ones that the French underground received from abroad throughout the war that had ended five years earlier.

The significance of mirrors and of mysterious phrases heard on the radio reaches its finality in the scene in which Eurydice is whisked back to Hades despite the efforts of Heurtebise to prevent Orphée from seeing her. As a culmination of the semicomic attempts they make to keep him from looking at her—the least convincing part of the movie—Orphée catches a glimpse of Eurydice in the rear mirror of the car when he is fiddling with its radio in the front seat and she is sitting behind him. Eurydice has contrived this return to the traditional versions of the myth because she recognizes how unreal the domestic situation has become between loving spouses who cannot speak face-to-face. The ending of the movie vindicates her belief while also retaining our usual feeling that a truly good marriage would find a way of dealing with all such impediments. Moreover, the conclusion is true to life inasmuch as the lovers who are only peripheral to the family—Death and Heurtebise—suffer greatly, as if in cosmic compensation for the happiness that the hero-artist and his wife may possibly attain.

When Cocteau reconceives and redirects all that in *The Testament of Orpheus,* he reiterates his frequently expressed idea about the thoughtlessness of mirrors and the need for them to reflect better. Amplifying the ambiguity of the word *reflect,* he says that mirrors ought to reflect more on the inability of their visual images to reflect reality as it is, if only because they distort it by reversing right and left. And though a mirror resembles the blank screen upon which movies are projected, our immersion in images that are either iconic or cinematic can always be deceptive. Engrossing as it is to see Cocteau die and then spring back to life, this effect makes sense—as he points out—only in relation to the recurrent deaths that he has experienced as a poet in the unpoetic circumstances of his actual existence. In that sense the poetry of film is never realistic, however much a poet or filmmaker may try to hide this fact about the nature of images.

Related thinking about the unreality of mirror images and their analogy to cinematic effects occurs in the puffs of smoke that accumulate at the beginning of *The Testament of Orpheus* and then take shape as a balloon before the credits appear. The puffs of smoke are the filmmaker's musings and vague impressions, which he has fashioned into a work of art that he will now present to us as an object lighter than air but complete within its membrane. At the end of the movie the balloon is burst by a pointed instrument in the hand of the filmmaker, and puffs of smoke replace it as a way of indicating that what we saw was all incorporeal, just thin air and figments of some masterful construction as Prospero says in *The Tempest*.

The balloon itself is a suitable representation of the creativity in everything imaginative. In its roundness, it is a perfect enclosure from every spatial point of view; in its firmness and resilience, it has a separate though pliant material being of its own; in its buoyancy and seeming defiance of gravitational forces, it signifies artistic spirit's capacity to soar beyond humanity's plodding existence on earth. In *The Red Balloon* (1956), a short film in color made by Albert Lamorisse, twenty-five thousand balloons were needed to convey ideas not unlike the conception that Cocteau formulates in his brief inclusion of a single one in black-and-white. It shows aesthetic truth emanating out of imagination, which then rises above its origin in physical nature until it too is transcended, at least deflated, by a supervening reality—the sharpness of a detractor's evaluation, the fragility of all creative efforts, or just the sheer destructiveness of death that lurks within the destiny of everything that lives.

On his palette of pigments that may be suitable, Cocteau chooses material objects that are the same as the ones we ordinarily rely upon in life, except that his have magical properties. They attain their meaningfulness through their function in his narrative, rather than having a symbolic import of the sort that Glass describes, and that I have questioned. The white rose in *La Belle et la Bête* transforms itself into a white orchid in *The Testament of Orpheus.* As such, it is a work of art insofar as Cocteau tears it into tiny pieces and then reconstructs the flower in order to offer it to Minerva as a gift designed to win over her female sensibility. The harpoon with which the goddess nevertheless attacks him is indigenous to her mythic role as a huntress.

The gloves that enable Orphée to enter into the reality of the unreal are flexible plastic or rubber utensils like those a surgeon might use. In *La Belle et la Bête* they are hunting garments that a Prince Charming would wear out-of-doors and that the Beast also wears, since he is a predatory creature. The Beast gives one of his gloves to Belle in order to remind her of what he is and to facilitate her ability to return to him by merely wishing to do so. Through a kind of noblesse oblige, it also works in transporting her to her father when Magnifique is not available. The Beast tells Belle that he can trust her with the magic glove and the golden key to the treasure house, all his vital power residing in these objects, because he knows that her tender heart will bring her back and not let him die.

In the Orphic films there is no key, though keyholes exist in *The Blood of a Poet*. They represent differences between real and unreal that preclude any objective knowledge of either. In *The Testament of Orpheus* there is a horse, but it is totally unlike Magnifique and not white in color. Its blackness is coherent with the fearful zone the protagonist has now entered, and it consists of a cardboard head surmounting the body of a sinister-looking young man dressed in black. The eighteenth-century aristocrat played by Cocteau reaches this menacing atmosphere after having voyaged, magically but inaccurately, into the twentieth century. He arrives in the modern world wearing hunting gloves, but then leaves them behind. Does he do this out of forgetfulness, or as a commentary on our age? It doesn't matter since this final statement of Cocteau's myth, like the previous portions, is timeless: it belongs to all periods and is not limited to any single one.

That had been part of the introductory message appended at the beginning of *Orphée*. Cocteau there defends his right to bring this legend of ancient Greece into the present. In *The Testament of Orpheus*, whose science fiction narrative deals with the sheer possibility of time travel, Cocteau presents himself as a poet who lives simultaneously in the present, the past, and the future (except, as he says apologetically, he has a bad memory of the future).

This in turn pertains to Cocteau's blunder in *L'Eternel retour* about the meaning of Nietzsche's notion. The great myths do not belong to a transcendental realm beyond time, but they do return endlessly in various cultures. In the films of Cocteau, the recurrence of the myth of Orpheus is fascinating and worthy of repeated study because it reveals the progressive development of his own thinking. Being autobiographical in their filmed poetry, his films constitute a mythological time travel in a manner that differs from the one that Ovid, for instance, employs throughout.

Ovid could not avail himself of cinematographic imagery, and the religions his audiences presupposed were more attuned to primitive storytelling of the past than any in modern Western society. Ovid gives us a simple template that later generations have embellished in their own modality and developed art forms. Though using the language and the poetic devices of his time, he relies upon the narrative versions that were traditional in the ancient world. The Orpheus in Ovid's story of his metamorphosis is not a contemporary man, as he is in Cocteau's film. He is not a man at all, though mortal like one, but rather a lesser divinity capable of magical feats that set him apart from the rest of humanoid existence. When he descends into Hades, he is able to charm the ruling deities there because they naturally respond to his god-given talent as a poet and musician.

In his outcast state, and equally absolute for death, Dante must have identified with Ovid's Orpheus in the first part of his *Commedia*. Cocteau emulates Dante in *The Testament of Orpheus*, since he too travels back and forth to the infernal region, but Cocteau's exploration is quasi-scientific and not at all theological. Dante was engaged in a kind of space travel coherent with the doctrinal beliefs of the Middle Ages; Cocteau's time travel occurs within his professed ignorance of any cosmic or religious source that may operate in the existential realms he visits.

Ovid's stories are filled with references to the gods, and Orpheus is even identified as a son of Apollo and the muse Calliope. Though stripping away that genealogical paraphernalia, Cocteau also describes Orphée as a child of Apollo, the metaphoric and not literal god of poetry. Orphée descends into Hades without a magic-making lyre, but his exceptional genius puts him into a mythic category that other poets or musicians can hardly approximate. He is both "famous and unknown," the combination of which Cocteau considered the highest and best condition any person can achieve.

Still there is one human situation that Ovid's hero attains but that eludes Cocteau's. The fundamental premise in the Ovidian version is the fact that Orpheus really loves his wife—even to the point of excess. So great is his marital devotion that it alone prevents him from carrying out his intention of bringing Eurydice back to life. She dies a second time, while they are still en route out of the underworld, because Orpheus cannot control his adoration of her. Despite his having been told that he must not look at Eurydice before they get back home, he turns to gaze at his beloved. In the film, Orphée's love for his wife mainly appears in his being aggrieved when he first loses her and then overjoyed when he becomes a family man once again after she has been revivified by his efforts. His extramarital search for Death is more powerful and pervasive than this domestic motive. It is also more authentic for him as a poet who lives in a world that punishes its artists, one way or another, while also extolling their unmatchable creativity.

In Ovid the death of Orpheus occurs in a context that is unrelated to his love for Eurydice. He dies at the hands of the jealous and criminally insane Maenads, who hate him because he is oblivious to feminine charms. At this point Ovid describes Orpheus as a connoisseur of male beauty and a lover of boys. Though in the film Orphée is accidentally killed by a hostile crowd of men and women who suspect him of having murdered their friend Cégeste, his isolation and susceptibility to social condemnation is a state that Cocteau, a self-referential poet who was openly homosexual, understood full well.

As a modern artist who feels free to inject his personal experience into the myth he is refabricating, Cocteau differs from Ovid in other ways as well. The actors who play Orphée and Cégeste (Jean Marais and Edouard Dermit) were each intimate friends of Cocteau whose rivalry for his attention shows itself in at least one scene. This kind of subjectivity is inherent in Cocteau's conception of poetry, on the screen as on the printed page. Ovid's almost reverential rehearsal of a mythic text that derives from the professed objectivity of a communal religion is intentionally discarded. *Orfeu Negro* (*Black Orpheus*), the film that Marcel Camus made almost ten years later than Cocteau's, rectifies this deviation. Although it is completely modern and avoids any dependence upon magic and the unreal, it stays closer to Ovid's text and even gives most of the principal characters the same names.

In Camus' version the streetcar conductor who is also an award-winning singer and dancer in the Rio de Janeiro carnival festivities that dominate the entire film is named Orfeu. Having just learned about the classical myth of Orpheus, he chances to meet a beautiful young girl called Euridice. They do not get married, but their night of consummated lovemaking establishes them as a matrimonial pair. She has been fleeing an unacceptable suitor who threatens to kill her. He suddenly appears in the midst of the carnival, masquerading as Death. Trying to escape him, Euridice dies, not from a snakebite as in Ovid, but from something comparable—an electric wire that powers a streetcar.

Searching for her and hoping to restore her to life, Orfeu gets help from a cleaning man named Hermes; he confronts a vicious watchdog called Cerberus; and he descends into Hades in a magnificent shot that displays a broad and winding stairway that curves down and down and down within the interior of a five- or six-story building. He does not find Euridice there but only a Macumba ceremony devoted to the rites of the dead. Orfeu finally discovers his beloved lying on a slab in the city morgue. Carrying her back to the hillside shack in which they had made love, he is attacked by the wild, sex-driven women who have been spurned by him on previous occasions for various reasons, and above all now that his affections have been wholly directed toward Euridice. Staggering on the edge of a cliff with her body in his arms, he falls to his death while clutching her in a last embrace.

Though Camus' movie amplifies and renovates the Ovidian myth, it is presented from beginning to end as a realistic depiction of contemporary life and love. It therefore blends a typically modern legend of romance with a mythic tale and can be seen as an up-to-date rendition of Shakespeare's *Romeo and Juliet*. With their ability to represent and elicit erotic feelings in almost any audience, the great majority of films that have been made in the last hundred years have dealt with the travails of either those who are in love or those who would like to be. Cocteau's *Orphée* is not a romance, though it includes both the poet's reciprocal passion for Death and his erratic feelings about his wife. In its own way, Ovid presupposes the existence of each of these human states. In *Orfeu Negro* they provide the fundamental material out of which its glorification of Romantic ideas about sexual love is constructed.

In that regard Camus inserts a female love-object who has been rejected and whose uncontrollable jealousy activates the suspense we feel protectively in watching Euridice's flight from the death that pursues her. The rival woman, to whom Orfeu has given a wedding ring, does not kill the interloper in what she takes to be her marital relations, but she is the leader of the enraged women who become accessories to the death of Orfeu. This love triangle does not exist in Ovid. It has been included as a modern theme that all moviegoers can readily recognize.

The same might be said about the constant presence of frenetic dancing among the participants of the carnival, the singing by Orfeu and the other characters, and the bossa nova music that entranced audiences worldwide for decades after the film came out. However much Cocteau's version benefits from the music of Georges Auric in various places, we never see Orphée dance or sing, or even hear him read his poetry. Though he is highly productive, descended from Apollo in some sense or other, he is only a man who has to solve the human problems that are related to his being so great an artist. To that extent, though not in all its details, the creative spirit celebrated by the Ovidian myth is better served by Camus' movie.

As a means of expressing this aspect of the myth, Camus invents two new characters. They are young Brazilian boys who attach themselves to Orfeu and then to Euridice. One of them explains to the other that Orfeu is a wonder-worker whose singing and playing of the guitar causes the sun to rise each morning. In an early scene, we see Orfeu's guitar being passed from one person to another as he retrieves it from the pawnshop in which he left it until he can receive his streetcar wages. The guitar serves as a unifying icon that reveals the social and spiritual message of his calling.

After Orfeu's death, the two boys carry the instrument to a hillside just before dawn, and one of them improvises a song that he plays on it. Despite their grief in having lost Orfeu, their faith in the goodness of life and the natural sustenance of the sun is joyfully renewed. This is a happy outcome, more positive than the ending in either Ovid or Cocteau and more substantial than the moment of marital bliss that Cocteau threw in as the culmination of *Orphée*. In *The Testament of Orpheus*, there are no marriages, blissful or otherwise; and there is no rising sun as the evidence of any miracle that poetry or music or dance or some other art form can yield to make life worth living. And yet, despite his disillusioned posture, Cocteau also is celebrating the ineffable goodness of the aesthetic component in human experience. It is in fact the major message in all his filmic poetry.[18]

5

Mythmaking in Kubrick and Fellini

Appearing in 1968, Stanley Kubrick's *2001: A Space Odyssey* declares its mythic intentions in the subtitle itself. Just as we cannot mistake the fact that *Orphée* and *Pygmalion* originate in the myths that have come down to us through Ovid, so too do we recognize immediately the kinship between *2001* and the epic that Homer wrote. At the same time, Kubrick's title conveys an aura of academic or documentary research, as in the contents of a nonfiction book. The works of both Homer and Kubrick consist of voyages through unknown spaces enacted by a hero and his crew; the travel in each employs current modes of transportation available to the human race through the technology of the relevant period; and they culminate in a homecoming by the protagonist, who is the sole survivor of his adventures.

Kubrick's movie mainly occurs in the future, though only a little less than forty years later, while Homer's pertains to some undated era in the ancestral past. But that doesn't matter. The two of them are alike insofar as they contain cosmological as well as hero types of mythology. Homer presents the deities in scattered religions of the Greeks as characters who determine the course of his narrative about the heroic Odysseus.

He must cope with the hostility of Poseidon, partly on his own but also with the aid of Athena, and his final victory is an achievement that is personal as well as social and generically human. Having no belief about divinities such as those, and no anthropomorphic religion that might be similar, Kubrick constructs a new kind of pantheon related to the materialistic ideology of our present culture.

In one respect, however, Kubrick's effort is more mythological than Homer's. The voyage and return of the twenty-first-century hero delves into cosmic mysteries beyond anything envisaged by the story of Odysseus. There is no longer the motif of coming back to a wife and one's kingdom in Ithaca, or some other city, but rather the major theme is the discovery of humanity's place in the universe. Dave Bowman's mission ends with his being reborn as himself a demigod, a star-child or superlative superman in the making. Though *2001* begins with prehuman primates in their hostile terrain, we never see Dave's reentry into his native planet, or his ever having lived on it. Other than a couple of messages to and from family back home while the spaceship is in flight, and occasional communications from headquarters, the only creatures like ourselves that we see on earth are the ancestral apes fighting with each other or huddled in a cave and frightened by a storm outside.

The primate behavior represents our own condition as well, and in the same manner as the characters of Kubrick's other movies, both early and late. The normal state of homo sapiens is shown to be nasty, brutish, and infinitely aggressive. In the mythology of *2001* a new dimension arises, proclaimed by the fanfare of Richard Strauss's *Thus Spake Zarathustra.* It is an anthem for the benign aspiration to self-transcendence inherent in our technology at any level, however humble it may initially be. The fanfare is parodied in Jerzy Kosinski's satire *Being There* (1979) when the semidemented character played by Peter Sellers descends from protected seclusion and enters the slums and corrupt politics of Washington, D.C. Because of his simplemindedness, he is treated as a Zarathustra-like savior. In *2001*, the sequence with the primordial creatures ends when one of them, glorying in his acquisition of a more effective tool for destroying his enemies, throws the wondrous object he has found—a bone of some other animal—into the air. The camera turns it into a spaceship serenely voyaging to the moon.

Not just in Méliès's fantasy but throughout the centuries, a trip to the moon has resided within a region of human imagination that is able to contemplate the pleasures and the challenges to be found on that celestial body. For Kubrick it is just a way station on a path that leads beyond our solar system. As we learn, a black monolith that is identical with the one we saw in the primate scenes has been found on the moon. We infer that the developmental distance between the primitive beasts and the greatly evolved human beings who have managed to defeat terrestrial gravity must somehow result from whatever powers are embedded in these monoliths. Thereafter the narrative depicts the search for intelligent beings on Jupiter who have used it to transmit radio waves to this local area in space.

Thirty-five years after Kubrick and Arthur C. Clarke had written the screenplay for the movie, out of which Clarke then made a novel based on it, he quotes Kubrick as having said: "What I want is a theme of mythic grandeur."[1] What Kubrick got and gave us was a film that differs from any usual adaptation inasmuch as 40 percent of it is silent. Even the words of a narrator, which Kubrick had included at first, are entirely absent. Though his movie is a work of science fiction, it is a product that only motion pictures can fabricate. In being simultaneously a visual and literary artifact, it illustrates—like most of the subsequent science fiction films that have capitalized on its enormous success—how greatly the purely visual can tell the story and retain our interest without needing more than a minimum of spoken continuity.

There is, however, a price that the filmmaker must pay for that mode of presentation. While the succession of engrossing images in *2001* is mesmerizing and increases the suspenseful unfolding of the plot, it also diminishes the cognitive dimensions of the underlying myth. In more than one place, Kubrick insists that he wished to reach the "subconscious" of a viewer, which he sometimes refers to as his or her "emotional" state, and he claims that this requires an avoidance of the rationality in ordinary life. "I tried to create a visual experience, one that bypasses verbalized pigeonholing and directly penetrates the subconscious with an emotional and philosophical content."[2] Various problems are related to this intention. For one thing, it depends on presuppositions—in Kubrick's case, specifically Freudian, as I will presently argue—that must be supported separately. Kubrick himself makes no such attempt, and neither does he justify his assumption that the subconscious, whatever it may be, is the same as the emotional.

The most interesting discussion of this issue occurs in an interview that appeared in *Playboy* shortly after *2001* was released. In that exchange Kubrick appears extremely well informed about recent research in aeronautical astronomy, space travel, and the possibility of life in other parts of the universe. He reveals a largeness of intellect that few other filmmakers can possibly match. But his own ideas, in most fields, seem amateurish and unformed. That does not affect his capacity as a mythmaker or one who sought for mythic grandeur in *2001* and other films. But it is a key to understanding what constitutes the mythology that he created in this work.

In the course of the *Playboy* interview, Eric Nordern asks Kubrick how he can account for the hostile reception that New York film critics bestowed upon *2001* at its premiere. In Nordern's words they felt it should be "exempted from the category of art . . . [and] castigated it as dull, pretentious, and overlong."[3] Kubrick replies by suggesting that "perhaps there is a certain element of the lumpen literati that is so dogmatically atheist and materialist and Earth-bound that it finds the grandeur of space and the myriad mysteries of cosmic intelligence anathema."[4] Though the film attests to the fact that Kubrick's imagination is certainly not earthbound, his own views are typically scientistic and materialist as well as tritely atheistic. The extent and the limitations of his thinking appear in responses that he later gives to Nordern's questioning.

When Kubrick is asked whether he agrees with critics who consider *2001* "a profoundly religious film," he states: "I will say that the God concept is at the heart of *2001*—but not any traditional, anthropomorphic image of God. I don't believe in any of Earth's monotheistic religions, but I do believe that one can construct an intriguing *scientific* definition of God, once you accept the fact that there are approximately 100 billion stars in our galaxy alone, that each star is a life-giving sun and that there are approximately 100 billion galaxies in just the *visible* universe."[5] Having been challenged to show how this is relevant to his speculations about highly evolved biological species elsewhere in the universe, Kubrick says that since these other forms of life may have acquired powers beyond our comprehension they would be regarded as gods by lesser races such as ours. He concludes that "*anything* is possible, and it's unlikely that we can even begin to scratch the surface of the full range of possibilities."[6]

What I find crucial in this line of thought is the recurrent allusion to "possible" facts within the parameters of scientific (which is to say, empirical and technological) exploration. That in turn belongs to an ever-expanding realm within the imagination of our species. Kubrick is masterful in creating cinematic situations that awaken our desire to entertain such possibilities by treating them with a fidelity to detail that mimics what we experience daily in life on earth. Nevertheless, the ideas that might bolster adherence to the conclusions he suggests are almost totally absent. His talent consists in making fictional, and ultimately undefended, projections that draw upon commonplace beliefs—all of which may be justifiable perhaps—that he has glazed over with quasi-religious language conveniently supplied by our astounding imagination.

In that vein Kubrick, and many others, have interpreted this aspect of his endeavor as "spiritual"—which is not the same as being religious while also allowing it to be considered "quasi-religious." Seductive as this range of terminology may be, its cash value resides in the mythological nature of filmmaking itself that I have been discussing throughout this book. Before analyzing the mythic scope that pervades *2001* and other Kubrick films, it will be useful to compare the creative mentality in them with the opposing type that results in the achievements of Federico Fellini. The two great filmmakers are very different, and yet also alike in ways that warrant investigation.

The nearest that Fellini comes to matters of space travel occurs in *8½*. The beleaguered film director in it is trying to complete a movie about efforts to leave this planet after a nuclear holocaust has occurred. We see the scaffolding for the launch pad at the beginning of the movie and then in scenes toward the end. The actual takeoff is aborted because the movie in the movie is itself scratched. At his wit's ends throughout *8½*, the director finally gives up on the project and cancels all further shooting for it. In that sense, Fellini's character having failed and his dreams of space travel disintegrating, Kubrick himself succeeds as a filmmaker who depicts a comparable enterprise in advanced stages of completion.

The famous opening sequence of *8½* prepared us for the movie's denouement insofar as what we observe is not only a dream but also a nightmare portraying one failure after another. At first the man who we later learn to be a director stifles from exhaust fumes that fill his car as it sits in a silent, eerie traffic jam. Then, when he somehow escapes from that, he floats through the air and soars beyond the clouds, with arms outstretched like the statue of Christ at the beginning of *La Dolce Vita*. Now, however, this embodiment of a savior is not held aloft triumphantly by a helicopter on its way to the Vatican. Instead he reaches a height along the sea tethered to the earth like a kite or balloon. At the other end of the rope, he is attached to a man who suddenly pulls him into a terrifying plunge. He falls like Icarus in Greek mythology, crashing down as punishment for having flown too close to the sun. This serves as the meaning of the nightmare, and as verification for the pervading anxiety in it that foreshadows the collapse of the director's plans for his film.

Though the contents of the movie within the movie never amount to anything, the greatness of *8½* results from its portrayal of the creative daydreaming of the director who thinks about episodes drawn from his past and present life that might contribute to this film. Fellini's cinematic skill is so accomplished in uniting these alternate presentations that we are never in doubt about their reality or irreality. The basic narrative itself is trivial and prosaic: the director has to deal with both his wife and his mistress, who hate each other, and who simultaneously visit him on the set in a counterproductive attempt to help him through his agony; the director has to negotiate with his producer and other coworkers by conning them as best he can about his nonexistent progress; he has to humor his actresses, whom he would rather dominate, as in the harem fantasy, as if he were their beloved master.

All this is projected as a movie about the life we know in everyday existence. Stylistically, it continues the neorealism in which Fellini's career began with films such as *I Vitelloni, Lo Sceicco bianco, La Strada,* and *Il Bidone*. Moreover, the notion of a spaceship leaving earth with survivors of a nuclear disaster reflects the fear-filled sensibility of many people in 1963, a year after the Cuban missile crisis. That alone could not sustain the shooting of *8½*, any more than the doomed movie within it, but it adds a useful background to Fellini's film. What makes the movie we do see so exceptional is something more than its paltry, though slightly engaging, realism. The sheer inventiveness of Fellini's cinematic imagination creates all the difference. It consists of two basic ingredients: first, the ability, the daring, the unrelenting courage to draw upon personal and normally private experiences of the filmmaker; and second, the implied assumption by him that he is a clown, as in the circus, and therefore that he can be truthful about his own life by providing the self-effacing and usually dismissive vision of the world that a clown purveys.

In films like *Amarcord* and *The Clowns*, these motifs supply the essential material with which Fellini's camera functions recurrently. In *8½*, however, the two elements assert themselves overtly as the guiding principles that inspire Fellini's narrative to proceed as it does from scene to scene. More than one critic has suggested that the movies of Fellini are more autobiographical than those of almost any other filmmaker. Fellini and Ingmar Bergman are akin in this respect. Perhaps that is why Bergman called him once his "fratello" (brother). Without jeopardizing the fictionality of their films, they both draw extensively from their off-camera existence. In Bergman, too, there is a fascination with clowns and with clowning. It is most explicit in the drama *Sawdust and Tinsel* (1953), but it also occurs in several of his comedies and even in *The Seventh Seal.* The painted white face of Death in that movie establishes him as some kind of clown, and the holy family perform on stage (also in whiteface) in a clownish manner. In Fellini this predilection merges with his self-referential tendency in a way that defines his genius and constitutes his mythological outlook. The entire world as he sees it, and as we watch it in the images he uses to represent it, is a visual expression of both himself and his awareness of what it is be a clown. His imagination in film after film is entirely geared to that.

I think this may be what Bergman perceived and had in mind when he said: "I love his work and I love him as a person, if he is a person, which I doubt, because he has no limits; he's just like quicksilver—all over the place."[7] By extrapolating from this, one can see Fellini's output as a continuous attempt to present through his films the person that he really is and has been, as demonstrated by the autobiographical data to which he constantly reverts. It is therefore fitting that *8½* ends not only with the demolition of the director's plans about his space travel movie but also with scenes that come straight out of the circus. Having been dressed throughout his anguish in dark clothes, the director appears in a white suit that signifies the gaiety of his newfound freedom while also attesting to his status as the leading clown. He stands on a small stage and directs a musical marching band of four other clowns (also dressed in white), on parade and playing a quirky lighthearted circus tune by Nino Rota.

At the same time the director orchestrates a long line of actors and members of the crew who walk and then run in a large circle, as members of a circus do at the end of a performance. They are no longer the characters we have seen, or the crew that has been filming them, but rather real men and women showing their stuff before the camera and proud of what they have done as professionals. They are the people who evoke and relive what Fellini, like the director of the aborted movie, has imaginatively chosen to include in the making of a work of art. *8½* can end on this high note of aesthetic achievement, instead of desperation, since the display of personal failure has elicited Fellini's ability to fulfill the two impulsions that have predominated from the start. In effect he is saying: You see, it's all been clownishness and that's what I, Federico Fellini, am in myself.

In a documentary called *Federico Fellini's Autobiography*, he is quoted as having remarked about *Lo Sceicco bianco* (1952): "I wasn't trying to prove anything. I have no message for humanity. I'm sorry. In all sincerity, I was trying, first and foremost, to make an entertaining film. Actually, I wanted to entertain myself. You see—and I hope no producers are listening—I think of films as wonderful toys, marvelous pastimes."[8] The truth in this confessional applies to all of Fellini's movies. While retaining a background of verismo in keeping with his neorealistic origins, they revel in large numbers of bizarre and sometimes grotesque characters whose antics are not only amusing in themselves, as in a circus, but also representative of what Fellini called "the vivid confusion of life."[9] With his great storehouse of cinematic effects, Fellini regales us with images that may pretend to be derived from thoughts or dreams the characters undergo within their narratives but are really testaments to the filmmaker's own imagination. If there is mythic grandeur in Fellini's work, it consists in the grandeur of that.

Giulietta degli spiriti (1965) is a good example of what I mean. In the context of a pedestrian housewife's suspicions about her husband's sexual infidelity, we observe social events that dazzle us with the rapid overlays of conversation by outlandish men and women. Their hectic verbal exchanges, speeded up as if to emphasize the absurdity in what they say to each other, are somewhat boring intrinsically. But then they lead into magnificently constructed fantasies more or less pertaining to Giulietta's psychological crisis. How she recovers from it is never explained, but we do not care. What has enchanted us throughout the film is the demonstration of Fellini's imagined varieties of sights and sounds that are coherent with *her* imaginings when she is either awake or asleep. In Fellini's hands the camera articulates in a very original way the myth of imagination itself as a supreme and all-justifying phenomenon that exists for its own sake, and as a creative force throughout human life as a whole. His celebration of it is a triumphant display that reverberates and remains endlessly enjoyable.

Satyricon, Fellini's loose adaptation of the novel by Petronius, he cogently describes as "a science-fiction picture in a sense." Assuming that we really know very little about life in ancient Rome, he unites this fact to his own condition as someone in the present creating a cinematic story about the past: "I felt a bit lost, but I feel that the healthiness of these adventures rests on looking into the complete obscurity in myself. I understood that the real key to making this picture was this unknown dimension." Fellini then explains his calling *Satyricon* science fiction by stating: "Science fiction is something that we don't know because we don't know what has been lost or, at any rate, what is unknown."[10]

This sense of the "complete obscurity in [himself]" provides the mythological authorization of Fellini's imaginings. At the end of the interview from which I have been quoting, he remarks: "I am not a movie director who consciously plots the movements of the camera, because they are very natural. Imagination is everything. The picture is in my head, and I just try to make it."[11] This in turn reinforces his belief that "it is absolutely impossible not to be autobiographical. I think that *Satyricon* is maybe much more autobiographical than *8½* because it is not an adapted biography. But maybe the anguish, the fear, the faith, the atmosphere that is in *Satyricon*, maybe that has to do with myself in a more immediate way."[12]

At the same time, Fellini's type of mythmaking does not prevent him from having at least one message he's always ready to impart. He is highly scornful in his later work of the tasteless and insidious outpouring of television as a rival form of entertainment. In addition to sarcastic short films to that effect, his *Ginger and Fred* is largely a polemic against this new development in Italian culture. But there, also, Fellini's predominant perspective takes over in the course of that effort. The movie begins with the spectacle of freakish people who are assembling for a television program and are then subjected to the chaos of their disorganized rehearsals. Having been delighted by the amusing nonsense of it all, we finally view the show itself, virtually from the beginning to the end. In it the strange characters behave like dedicated and seasoned professionals, clownish as required on occasion but not at all freakish, and quite successful in their authentic desire to please the live audience. In his love of entertainment as such, Fellini cannot refrain from making an artistic reenactment of their performance. He thereby undercuts his general derision of television shows geared to a low level of mass receptivity. His preconceived message succumbs before this opportunity to employ, once again, his manifold and limitless powers of creative imagination.

In Kubrick the myth of imagination operates in another way. He and Fellini are alike in their total reliance upon aesthetic inventiveness as a cardinal resource in human nature, but they are completely disparate in their interpretation of what this involves. Playful as Kubrick's directing is, the absurdity of its clowning is not designed as autobiographical diversion. Though his personal vision permeates his work, it never turns that into self-reflective entertainment. Kubrick and Fellini elucidate each other's talents as contrasting, rather than similar, masters of their trade.

In saying this, I realize that in Kubrick's films clowning continually occurs. In *Dr. Strangelove or: How I Learned to Stop Worrying and Love the Bomb,* the antics of General Buck Turgidson, as played by George C. Scott, are performances straight out of the circus. He even does an accidental backflip that corresponds to the wrongheadedness of his reasoning. In *A Clockwork Orange,* Malcolm McDowell's cavorting from start to finish resembles the shticks that clowns in vaudeville might use on stage in imitation of a circus. His name alone is risible: Alex DeLarge, though he has none of the majesty of Alexander the Great. As if it were the straight man in each of his exploits, Kubrick's camera revels in the outrageous aspect of every scene. As a spoof of comedic silent films that make us laugh at the magical speeding up of reality, it even shows in very rapid motion the overt sex with the young girls whom Alex has picked up. Accompanied by the pounding rhythm of "The William Tell Overture," the filming condenses the many acts of fornication, and the repeated dressings and undressings, into events that are funny because devoid of recognizable feeling, and as mechanical as the camera itself. In *The Shining,* when the Jack Nicholson character goes berserk, he insanely parodies the TV announcer Ed McMahon introducing Johnny Carson. He fiendishly grimaces as he says, *"Heeere's Johnny!"*

In these, and many other instances of Kubrick's coruscating wit, the effect is very different from the clowning in Fellini. That constantly remains a self-deprecatory and often sad enunciation of the director's feelings about the lack of meaning in his own life. In the case of Kubrick, nothing of the sort appears, for the simple reason that Kubrick never reveals himself. He communicates his humor, and whatever ideas about the world he may have, through the camera that hides him from us. He really *is* a camera, as in the title of the play and then movie adapted from Christopher Isherwood's *Goodbye to Berlin*. In all his productions, Kubrick was a director who also did the cinematography, or else supervised it very closely. He began his career as a news photographer and retained the mentality suitable for that occupation throughout his life.

The first rule of news photography is *Get the facts!* Which is to say, remain faithful to the visual appearance of reality, and as evidence of something that has happened in a particular place at a particular time. This alone tells us much about the "mythic grandeur" that Kubrick wanted for *2001*. The event that would occur in that year is presented as a great, perhaps the greatest, occurrence in human history. Though our primate ancestors could not comprehend the first magic monolith, it symbolized the search for life that has motivated the progress of mankind and the growth of its varied civilizations. And of great importance in Kubrick's conception is the notion that the ultimate completion of this process takes place in the proximate future.

Since the future is always a blank until it becomes the present, virtually anything can happen then. All the optimism and hopefulness that people have felt devolve from that unverified belief. What is truly mythic about Kubrick's vision in *2001* manifests his faith in the boundless opportunities for exploration that await us in the coming years. The astronauts, above all Dave Bowman as their leader, are equivalent to the pioneers whom Americans have idealized in film and story as the founders of what became the United States.

Kubrick's epic must therefore be categorized with the many films—those of John Ford, for instance—that have helped create the myth of the West, how it was won and settled through the bravery and futuristic commitment of heroic men and women. Earth having been conquered and ravaged since then, their descendants turn to outer space as the reality about which contemporary imagination can now construct a viable mythology. In documenting this, Kubrick remains the news photographer who learned his craft by snapping arresting shots for magazines like *Newsweek* and *Look*. The picturing of fictional space travel in the twenty-first century would have to be as precise and as graphic as illustrations for these periodicals.

Approaching Kubrick's mythmaking from this point of view, we can well argue that all his films fit a similar pattern. A great deal of the power and grim propulsion in *Dr. Strangelove*, for example, comes from the business with the dials and exact protocols on the airship that will finally deliver the devastating bomb. The same holds for the detailed routine for confirming the contents of the crew's emergency equipment. It causes us to feel that this is what would really be done by servicemen in that situation and at that moment. It is a ritual whose absolute realism seduces our imagination into accepting this as a possible scenario for the final calamity. In being so conscientious about the correctness of their behavior, the crewmen seem to be truly intent upon carrying their suicidal mission to its mythically ordained conclusion.

Therein lies the horrible absurdity that Kubrick wants to undermine by subjecting it to the contrary absurdity that resides in his kind of sardonic humor. Though *2001* is neither sardonic nor humorous, Kubrick's depiction of the minutiae of daily life in an interplanetary rocket ship relies upon the same technique. Our spectatorial involvement is thereby lured into believing that the imminent reality will be comparable. In its subtle, and often soundless, dependence upon the visual, *2001* is thoroughly convincing. Previous science fiction movies had none of this representational expertise.

Because the frequent absence of conversation works so well in *2001*, continuous discussion or a narrative voiceover would have diminished, not augmented, the film's persuasiveness. While we observe the spaceship from the exterior, as it glides through the blackness of the firmament, we hear the gracious and soothing strains of "The Blue Danube Waltz." This sonic effect is not descriptive; rather, it superimposes a sense of lulling and supportive assurance. The combination of sight and sound makes the optimistic mythmaking irresistible.

At first glance the structure of the plot seems straightforward and easy to follow. In the beginning, at the origin of humanity, there is primitive creativity somehow related to the brute aggressiveness that is characteristic of our species. At the end, we are captivated by the prospect of a new and peaceful race of supermen generated from the star-child pictured in its fetal stage. On the voyage, we see the mythic oneness of buddies united in a joint pursuit, together with secondary comrades waiting in hibernation until they are needed.

The survivor of this trip that no other human beings had ever made surmounts the perils of space travel and also the rebellion of a social subordinate. Though Hal has cognitive abilities superior to Dave and Frank, he belongs to the lower class of beings that are mechanical rather than organic. In the television interview soon after liftoff, Dave says Hal is just another member of the crew, and so great is his reliability that he is treated as if he were an equal. But he is nevertheless a servant who does not have the same rights and privileges as his masters, not even a right to exist beyond the time that he remains useful to them.

In keeping with this persona, Hal's voice is always unctuous and self-denying. Its quiet and creamy timbre resembles the voice of a preacher whose cunning one might suspect straightaway. Nevertheless, he emerges as the first computer slave of his genus to malfunction or misbehave as he does. He is himself a mythically heroic figure. He is a Spartacus of his electronic people, and the movie about the anti-Roman insurgent that Kubrick directed in part as a hired substitute may have spawned that conception of the wayward computer in *2001*.

In a manner that is perfect for this plot, the overly compliant voice that Kubrick has given Hal coheres with stock portrayals of a villain in B movies. Since Hal is the only true intellectual in his film, Kubrick was also drawing upon the typical American animosity toward mad scientists and corruptible geniuses. At the same time, we in the audience are initially charmed by this example of a wholly serviceable machine that talks like a human being and plays winning matches like a chess master (which Kubrick was himself). Until we learn differently, we see Hal as an ancestor of R2-D2 and C-3PO, the likable droids in *Star Wars* (1977). The three of them seem to show unstinted good will toward lesser creatures like us. Once Hal has defected to the dark side, we recognize that except for his natural and normal fear of annihilation he is a kind of psychopath, and hence affectively deficient.

Beyond these dramatic components, it would be unreasonable to interpret Kubrick's narrative as an important probing into the relationship between technology and the modern version of human nature. His work yields little, if any, insight into problems of that kind. In being a bad guy whose astounding capacity for goodness we greatly admire, Hal, as well as his discontents, belongs to the category of magical marvels that all mythic fantasies, including cosmological ones like Kubrick's, introduce for the sake of impressing us with their exciting wonderment. In that regard, Hal is a special effect comparable to the alignment of earth, moon, and sun that precedes the appearance and activation of the black monoliths. This celestial conjunction is presented as a bit of astronomical magic that furthers the myth, and at momentous occasions in the tale fortifies our aesthetic acceptance of its cosmic realism. To infer any further meaning would be unwarranted.

Instead of having a plethora of ideas, Kubrick manifests a considerable degree of cleverness in addition to his superb technical facility. In *2001* the dominant man-ape who sees the first black monolith reaches out and touches it with his finger. The gesture may well be interpreted, as it has been by at least one commentator, as a reference to Michelangelo's Adam extending his finger to receive life from God in the mural on the ceiling of the Sistine Chapel.[13] When Dr. Floyd approaches the second monolith, in the Clavius plain on the moon, he also uses a finger to make contact. But now, with four million years of evolution having elapsed since the first one appeared, the finger is enclosed in Dr. Floyd's thickly insulated glove. At the very end, when a severely aged Dave Bowman is about to be born again as the star-child, from his deathbed he points his outstretched finger at the monolith before him. Kubrick zooms in on it to tell us that the cosmic consummation has been attained.

Kubrick's employment of the "World Riddle" theme from Strauss's *Thus Spake Zarathustra* is rightly thought to be one of the most brilliant musical devices in the history of film. It occurs several times in *2001* as an accompaniment to the black monoliths and their mission on the earth, on the moon, and then beyond Jupiter. In Strauss's tone poem, the allusion to the Nietzschean idea of the superman is likewise applicable. But the movie makes no attempt to consider the implications that Nietzsche built into this word—for instance, his emphatic assertion that the nature of the superman is to be found in artistic creativity as contrasted with Germanic or any other militarism.

This omission need not be deemed a failing on Kubrick's part. There is no supervening need for him to burden his spectacular with fundamental questions of that sort. It is worth noting, however, that whatever the differences in subject matter between him and Fellini, his mythmaking—like Fellini's—remains largely confined to the surface values of cinematic visualization. It thus evades the crucial questions about ultimate reality that Kubrick, at least, pretends to engage. His blithe suggestion that superhuman beings *may* inhabit the universe and possess "limitless potentialities," including "the twin attributes of all deities—omniscience and omnipotence," seems empty and unpersuasive.[14] Despite its splendid technological veneer, the myth that Kubrick offers so inventively is far from being able to vindicate his claim to have formulated "an intriguing *scientific* definition of God."[15] Instead of bypassing reason and speaking directly to the subconscious, he ends up in an uncharted land of wish fulfillment.

In all of Kubrick's mythmaking there is no room for a heroic female. The hero is always a man, and usually one who is sullied by noxious forces that Kubrick depicts as basic in the material realities of our species. Prominent among them is sex and violence, which he presents with the detached fascination of a clinician or criminologist. Sustained by his meticulous and inspired cinematography, this combination of interests is very impressive in films like *The Killer's Kiss*, *The Killing*, and *Paths of Glory*. The intellectual thrust of these films reaches a higher level of achievement in *Lolita*, *Dr. Strangelove*, and *A Clockwork Orange*. In each of them, the nature of both sex and violence is shown from a somewhat different point of view.

Lolita begins with Humbert's murder of Quilty as an event whose instigation the rest of the movie explores through a prior account told to us by Humbert in a quasi-confession of his maniacal obsession. He portrays himself as a sex-driven man who is willing to marry a woman he abhors in order to remain close to her teenage daughter, the object of desire that he stalks throughout the film. As in Proust and the Nabokov text that became the modified source of the screenplay, Humbert's need to retain and possess Lolita is intensified by her refusal to respond with any ardor. Male longing and pursuit is all we are given to inspect, and even that appears as an instinctual drive that includes little of the creativity that infuses human sexuality.

Part of the reason for this lies in the limited yet menacing censorship that curtailed what could be seen on-screen at the time, 1962. Production was held up because a Catholic board of review criticized, for example, the scene in which Humbert is engaged in foreplay with his wife but keeps looking at a small portrait of Lolita. The board complained that this undermined the sanctity of marriage. The scene remained in the final cut, but somewhat changed. More explicit sexuality or violence was taboo, and even the shooting of Quilty occurs when he is hiding behind a large painting and we cannot see his wounds or terminal agony. As a result, the movie focuses exclusively on a superficial showing of sex and violence, any love that the rival men may have felt for Lolita remaining unexamined, while its limited presentation of the primordial drives comes through as mainly cold and mechanistic.

By the time *A Clockwork Orange* was released in 1972, social mores had eased enough for Kubrick to exhibit graphically the viciousness in the psychopathic cruelty and rape of naked women that constitutes the delinquency of the juveniles in Anthony Burgess's novel. The moral issue that Kubrick dramatizes deals with the deleterious effects of tampering too radically with the inclination of males to vent their hostility toward society through criminal acts of sex and violence. Once Alex has been brainwashed by the shock treatment we see in great detail, he loses his vital energy. It returns when corrupt politicians and mindless public opinion forgive his past deeds, even treating him as a victim rather than a miscreant. From having been viewed as a hideous monster, he is suddenly treated like a noble survivor who believes in the love of mankind as embodied in Beethoven's Ninth Symphony. Alex's adoration of that music had appeared earlier in the movie as a paradoxical contrast to his vicious behavior. When his libidinal and aggressive appetites are restored in the happy conclusion designed to underline Kubrick's abomination of the social status quo, Beethoven's music blares forth as if in approval of the anarchistic message.

In *2001* there is no sex and, except for the man-ape mauling of a hapless opponent together with the slaughter of tapirs, no violence. When Hal kills the three hibernating scientists, he merely removes their life-support systems; and when he kills Frank, he deftly separates him from his umbilical tether. These acts are performed as sanitized and unemotional events. They constitute murder, but of a sort that is too passionless to express any of the hatred or physical mutilation we generally associate with violence.

The demolition of Hal is comparable in being a technological procedure as remote from a willed annihilation of life as switching off an electric light. Hal's remission step-by-step into lesser forms of digital experience is intriguing but hardly capable of eliciting feelings of compassion. We may be amused by his singing the popular love song "Daisy" toward the end, but the inherent poignancy of his demise can scarcely create much sympathy in us. The scene embodies the same irony as Alex's performance of "I'm singin' in the rain" while he batters the husband and prepares to rape the wife in *A Clockwork Orange.*

The two songs belong to the enormous body of literature that poets, mainly males, have created as a glorification of the supreme goodness in romantic love. That is a lofty castle in the air that our species has constructed over the morass of negative feelings intertwined in its biological program. If *2001* can be called "spiritual," it is because its usual adherence to the reductive view of life has transmuted the violence and sexuality of ordinary experience into the more splendid attainments that our evolved technology may someday achieve. The hopefulness is spiritual, but the causative attributes are not. When Hal and Dave play chess, it is the computer who wins. But when Dave dismantles Hal, he has checkmated him in a fashion that Kubrick could well have savored. Of greater significance is the fact that the analytical mind of Kubrick enables him to organize and to plot the minute opportunities afforded by the film equipment at his command. Through it he checkmates reality itself, and beyond the capacity of any board game.

❁

Warfare as a whole being a magnification of the aggressiveness in activities such as the playing of chess, *Dr. Strangelove* contains anomalies of this sort in several places. One is when we see Captain Kong ride his hydrogen bomb like a hobbyhorse into the Russian nuclear installation; another is when the idiotic sergeant reluctantly fires bullets into the vending machine whose coins will release the change that Captain Mandrake needs to call the White House, and then warns Mandrake that he'll have to answer to the Coca-Cola company for this; and finally, the last is a mano a mano demonstration of what it's all about, when General Turgidson wrestles the Russian ambassador, who is taking snapshots of the "big board," after which the president pompously chides them for fighting in the War Room (of all places!). As the sign on the army base insists, "Peace is our profession."

For its part, explicit sexuality is never shown in that movie, or only obliquely, as when Turgidson's girlfriend, in bed and scantily attired, moans suggestively that she isn't sleepy. The general, who has now been informed about the danger they are in, tells her that he'll just mosey over to the War Room to check out some things and that she should start her countdown, since he will be back before she can say "Blast off!" Without ever seeing his physical lovemaking, we recognize that for Turgidson this action is just an extension of his macho sensibility as a conquering warrior. We infer that the same is true of others in the chain of command. In the last moments of the film, even cold-blooded Dr. Strangelove gets aroused by the prospect of unbridled sex that will be available in their mineshaft to the male survivors of the holocaust.

This kind of sexual wit pervades *Dr. Strangelove* and elucidates its title. It is a strange love indeed that subordinates all erotic possibilities, whether libidinal or sensuous or romantic, to a desire to fight wars and kill other people instead of enjoying their company as fully as one can. In the 1960s the slogan "Make love, not war" served as a pacifist weapon against war itself. Kubrick enlarges that maneuver by portraying how not making love can lead to the self-defeating madness of nuclear suicide. His proof largely relies upon the inspired use of innuendoes and absurdist language about sex. By getting us to laugh, he rightly assumes, he may well cause us to understand what we truly want and how foolish the belligerent alternatives must be. Even the bonobos have learned that lesson, but human beings need to be kicked on their funny bone in the most imaginative fashion. Cinema is well equipped to do the job. Kubrick knew how to employ it in this capacity, better perhaps than anyone else.

In his review of *Dr. Strangelove,* Tim Dirks proffers an exhaustive catalog of the sexual references, sometimes subtle, sometimes gross, but always amusing, that give Kubrick's movie a kind of mythic grandeur of its own:

In addition to numerous sexual images and jokes throughout the film (including large phallic cigars, mating airplanes, guns, Ripper's impotent "loss of essence," and the orgasmic atom bomb that Kong rides between his legs) many of the absurd, omnipresent names of the male, military characters (caricatures) have sexual connotations or allegorical references that suggest the connection between war, sexual obsession and the male sex drive: [ten examples follow, the first of which is Jack D. Ripper, described as "a notorious English psychopathic killer of prostitutes, or a killer in general." Two others are: Buck Turgidson, "a 'buck' is a male animal or stud; 'turgid' means distended or swollen; and his delayed love-making to a real-life *Playboy* centerfold Tracy Reed—the *only* woman in the entire film"; and Merkin Muffley, the president, "merkin=slang for female pubic area or pudendum; muff=a woman's pubic area or genitalia, or specifically, the pubic hair / fur / wig for the female crotch."].[16]

Fellini films such as *La Dolce vita, Satyricon, Amarcord,* and *Ginger and Fred* also contain a great deal of sexual humor. But it is generally good-natured and lacking in any of the caustic overtones that Kubrick introduces to document the inescapable violence of sex. In their bland adherence to the idea that love and hate are inseparable and that by its very being love reduces to sexuality, the two filmmakers both accept the usual Freudian dogmas. They nevertheless differ in their interpretations of them. In Fellini one always senses the reverence that Italians have commonly bestowed upon mothers and male babies. The frequent male fascination with large-breasted women recurs in several of the Fellini films, reaching its peak in the more than comic scene of *Amarcord* when the boy voraciously sucks on one and then the other breast of the bountiful female who responds with profuse enjoyment that validates his ecstatic pleasure. In *Ginger and Fred,* among the performers preparing for the television show, there is a troupe of seventeen midgets and also an extremely large cow. Having examined the cow, one of the male midgets squeals with great excitement that she has eighteen nipples and therefore they can all suckle her at the same time.

This kind of frivolity about reproduction and the nurturance of the young exists in none of Kubrick's films. His mythology ignores such matters, with the possible exception of the image of the star-child's fetus in its sac, which seems as large as the earth itself in the closing frame of *2001.* But that mythic being who will somehow turn into a super-Christ issues from no madonna and peers at us with eyes that are too big to be human. From this terminating shot, we can hardly make any inferences about affective attachments, whether desirable or undesirable. In *Eyes Wide Shut* (1999), his last film, Kubrick did, however, seem to be searching for some clarification about the nature of love in relation to sexuality.

Ever since the 1970s Kubrick had wanted to adapt Arthur Schnitzler's novel *Dream Story*. When he finally did so, just before he died, his film had a very mixed reception. In its general conception, and specifically in its including female (but not male) nudity, it was dismissed out of hand by many who called it anachronistic—made twenty-five or thirty years too late. Some critics did consider it a fitting culmination to his life's work, but mainly because of its daring cinematography and realistic use of shocking obscenities, which in fact were no longer shocking to its likely audiences.

I see it as an extension of Kubrick's mythological approach to aspects of marital intimacy that he had largely neglected before. *The Shining*, based on Stephen King's novel, prominently featured the little family that lives through the frightening unfolding of their horror story. In it the Nicholson character is a kind of psychotic inversion of the mythically heroic male. But we are told very little about his private feelings toward his wife, played by Shelley Duvall. In the Schnitzler novel that aspect of married life was the focus of attention, its narrative progression being developed in dreams as well as conscious events intermeshed with them. The dreams are never presented directly by the narrator himself, but only through descriptions that the husband and wife give each other. The challenge for Kubrick was to render the sleeping states, as well as the interspersed world in which they exist, through images that are both dreamlike and realistic at the same time. In doing so, he uses effects of sight and sound that yield the same eerie atmosphere as in *The Shining,* but now much less surreal and more greatly akin to perceptions in daily experience.

In the Schnitzler text, there are places that make the reader wonder whether the entire narrative is the telling of a dream. For instance, when the protagonist, Fridolin, leaves the mysterious house of carnal indulgence, he is taken back to the city in a coach from which he cannot escape. Despite his frantic attempts, he is unable to open either the right- or left-hand door. The carriage stops abruptly in a deserted area, both doors spring apart simultaneously, he alights without knowing where he is, and the coach then drives off "through the open fields into the night."[17] This sense of dreamlike uncanniness permeates the novel and is captured in Kubrick's movie by the fairly unrealistic shots of nighttime streets, presumably in New York, and through the use of pinging, sharp and high-pitched, notes strategically placed in Gyorgy Ligeti's background music. What is lost, however, is Schnitzler's insight into the mentality of the main character.

In the Kubrick version, his name is Dr. Bill Harford. He is played by Tom Cruise with less than total success. In both the story and film, we follow the protagonist in his odyssey of nocturnal adventures that are fundamentally, though often covertly, sexual. In an early scene Bill is stunned by the revelations of his wife Alice (Nicole Kidman) about unfulfilled desires she has had toward a stranger. During his wanderings away from her and what she has told him, Bill keeps having flashes of jealous images, filmed in grayish black-and-white in this otherwise brightly colored film. We see his thoughts of Alice having sex with the man she mentioned, but we are not provided with the actual jealousy, the jealous feelings and ideas, that are coursing through his mind and that Schnitzler describes very carefully. That alone changes the nature of the odyssey. In Kubrick it is more or less reduced to a man's hunger for extramarital experience as occasioned by his wife's having wounded his male vanity. In Schnitzler the situation has much further implications.

I can best illustrate this by quoting a passage that presents Fridolin's cogitation about the weird night he has just had and that ended with his being "redeemed" by a naked beauty in the house from which he has been expelled: "And he vowed not to rest until he had again found the beautiful woman, whose dazzling nakedness had so intoxicated him. Only now did he think of Albertine [his wife's name in the novel]—and even so he felt as though he was obliged to conquer her as well, as though she could not, should not be his again until he had betrayed her with all the others he had met that night."[18]

These other women are willing sex partners whose overtures the doctor has declined. Encounters with them, or their equivalents, also appear in the film and remain equally unconsummated, but without the doctor's thoughts about these experiences. Also omitted is Schnitzler's description of his final awareness of what his wife really means to him. In the novel the process begins after he reads a newspaper story about the death by poisoning of a young woman who, he thinks, might be the beauty that saved his life. He decides to visit the corpse in the mortuary, but then realizes that her face was veiled and would be unrecognizable except for "the eyes—eyes which were now extinguished."[19] Reflecting on this, he concludes that "ever since he had first read the notice in the paper he had imagined the faceless suicidal woman as having Albertine's features, indeed, as he now realized with a shudder, his wife had been incessantly hovering before his eyes as the woman he was seeking."[20]

Schnitzler's text is likewise mutilated by Kubrick's handling of the scene in which the husband returns home, awakens his wife from a nightmare she has had, and gets her to disclose its contents. In the movie version, her account finishes with her painful memory of having submitted in the dream to sexual intercourse with a horde of men who were using her as a common whore. Since this is what happens to all the beautiful women in the enchanted castle that the husband had visited, Kubrick is obviously linking this strange coincidence to the sheer fantasy of Bill's night on the town. In Schnitzler the wife's statement is a lengthy and extremely convincing revelation not only of her ongoing desire for the stranger she had told Fridolin about, but also of her having sex with that man in her dream while Fridolin was being tortured by some cruel princess because he insisted on remaining true to his wife "until all eternity."[21]

As if to compensate for these deletions and the consequent minimalization in the depth of the narrative, Kubrick enriches it with the visual allure of the naked women. He also depicts Alice as a much more liberated person than the character is in the novel. In Kidman's enactment, Alice is not fully emancipated but well on the way to that. The first time we see her she is dressing for the grand party to which she and Bill have been invited. In the privacy of their apartment, her preparations are routine and unerotic. While she is on the toilet, Bill shows no interest in her body. He hardly takes notice of it, and she makes no attempt to cover her seminudity.

As a counterpoint to this scene of familial domesticity, Bill will later become an observer of the gorgeous nudes who participate in the ritual at the magic castle, so unlike the one in Cocteau's

La Belle et la Bête. That one sustained a myth of pure love; the rites and formal mythology of this one celebrate unfettered sexuality. At the same time, the unimpassioned orgies that are discreetly shown serve as a commentary upon the institutional sex that is legitimized by marriage and, at its best, eventuates in marital oneness. The password to the public privacy upon which Bill intrudes is "Fidelio," the title of Beethoven's mythic opera—the greatest opera ever written about married love.[22]

Yielding to the commands intoned by a head priest in the presence of a congregation whose members are all wearing masks and formal cloaks, the naked women silently do what they are told to do. Having been instructed, they pair off with men as they would in a brothel. Kubrick allows us to see all this beyond anything Schnitzler or even a modern novelist could portray in words. The prior sequence in the apartment he amplifies by including brief scenes with the couple's daughter, who needs a sitter while the parents are out together, as well as other such accoutrements to life in Manhattan.

In bringing Schnitzler up-to-date, Kubrick alters the kind of language that the characters speak. They use the common obscenities to which I referred, but also there are other notable variations in the exchange between husband and wife when their matrimonial reconciliation is attained. Schnitzler closes his story as follows:

"Now we are truly awake," she said, "at least for a good while." He wanted to add: forever, but before he had a chance to speak, she laid a finger on his lips and whispered as though to herself: "Never enquire into the future."

And so they both lay there in silence, both dozing now and then, yet dreamlessly close to one another—until, as every morning at seven, there was a knock upon the bedroom door and, with the usual noises from the street, a triumphant sunbeam coming in between the curtains, and a child's gay laughter from the adjacent room, another day began.[23]

Kubrick's ending is of another sort:

Alice The important thing is we're awake now and hopefully for a long time to come.
Bill Forever.
Alice Forever?
Bill Forever.
Alice Let's . . . let's not use that word, it frightens me. But I do love you and you know there is something very important we need to do as soon as possible.
Bill What's that?
Alice Fuck.[24]

The title Kubrick gives to his last film proclaims an idea he had long held but never fully developed before. When eyes are wide open, we get information we need for living in the real world; when they are shut, we dream and have fantasies. In his art as a filmmaker, Kubrick experimented with ways in which the two conditions may be not only combined but also harmoniously integrated. The dreaming and fantasizing then become mythological vehicles that enliven reality, which movies do not, cannot, duplicate but can possibly transform into aesthetic truthfulness. Far from excluding reality, eyes that are *wide* shut employ its contents as a photographer's viewfinder does.

Having successfully confronted their interpersonal problems through ordeals they overcame, Bill and Alice have been engaged in a myth about marriage much as Tamino and Pamina are in Mozart's *The Magic Flute*. They utter the words of their happy ending at Christmastime in a store where they are buying presents for their daughter. She gets the teddy bear she wanted, after Alice makes sure the price is right. This tells us that the American mythos of family happiness is now totally satisfied.

By defining love in terms of sexuality, Kubrick remains faithful to the philosophical orientation of Schnitzler's fiction. Max Ophüls does so as well in *La Ronde*, his cinematic rendition of Schnitzler's play with the same title. In it all the characters enact a posy ring as both recipients of sex and as transmitters of it to the next man or woman in the chain, starting with the prostitute played by Simone Signoret and ending with Gérard Philippe (the count). We never learn whether they are united by some venereal disease they have now passed on to one another. That is not the point of Schnitzler's play or Ophüls's movie. Instead the instinct in itself pervades and dramatically dominates both works as the Schopenhauerian force of nature that joins male and female into a unified, or at least integrated, state of being. The same mythic attachment is expressed in the ironic song about intersexual oneness that Richard Wilbur wrote for Leonard Bernstein's *Candide*, except that there it is indeed syphilis or gonorrhea that each person gives to his or her libidinal partner.

The mythology of both *Eyes Wide Shut* and *Dream Story* is of another type. In glorifying the possible goodness and all-inclusive mystery of human sexuality, they simultaneously subsume it within the myth of the Wandering Jew or Flying Dutchman. As in Wagner's Romantic opera, the searching, and to that degree heroic though basically evil, male travels through the world in the hope of finding a beautiful woman who will release him from his miserable condition by dying because of love for him. When the protagonist finds her, the two die together in a Liebestod, a mingling of love and death, that establishes the linchpin of a mythological merging between them. As a variation of this theme, Verdi's *Rigoletto* introduces a motif that derives from the perspective of Christian saintliness. In the purity of her love, Gilda gives her life to save the lascivious man who has betrayed and even raped her. This is only a partial Liebestod: the female's love leads to her death but the beneficiary of it, the duke, never merges with her. He stays on earth and continues to follow his wicked ways.

Though the religious message of these versions is secularized by Kubrick as well as Schnitzler, its idealistic components remain as a determining motif that propels the perilous adventures of Fridolin / Bill Harford within his bourgeois and contemporary milieu. In both Schnitzler's novel and Kubrick's film, the male protagonist fails in his attempt to learn the identity of the beauty who has offered to sacrifice herself. His quest is fruitless, even in the mortuary to which he travels like Orpheus seeking Eurydice among the dead in Hades. In the Kubrick movie, the plot is tidied up with the invention of the character Ziegler. At the beginning he procures Bill's medical help with an unclothed woman who has overdosed on drugs and passed out in his mansion. At the end Ziegler tells Bill that the woman he has been looking for is the same person, a suicidal hooker who didn't die for him as he had come to think but rather because she could no longer live with her drug habit.

That deflationary explanation eliminates the transcendental underpinning of both the Wagnerian and the Verdian myths, and in Kubrick as in Schnitzler the husband goes back to his wife with a feeling that their marital relationship has been strengthened by the bizarre but cathartic experiences they have endured. He has been unmasked as one who tries to alleviate his middle-age frustration through sexual wandering, incomplete as it may be. Finding on his side of the bed the mask he had worn that night but lost, he bursts into tears and makes a confession to his wife that is parallel to her earlier depiction of her erotic dream. This reunites them and thereby completes the mission of the mythology. Whether the hero is Odysseus or Dave Bowman or Bill Harford, the history of his voyaging ends in revealing home truths about himself and his masculinity within a trajectory that returns him to the wife, the family, the country, or the planet to which he rightly belongs.[25] At our present level of development, film—by itself and through its interaction with other art forms—serves as the most advanced mode of making and perpetuating myths of that sort.

Notes

Introduction: Philosophical Dimensions of Myth and Cinema

1. For further discussion of related elements in Bergson's philosophy, see the chapter "Sympathetic Intuition: Henri Bergson," in my book *Explorations in Love and Sex* (Lanham, Md.: Rowman & Littlefield, 2001), 169–197.

1 *The Lady Eve*

1. James Harvey, untitled essay in *The Lady Eve*, DVD, directed by Preston Sturges (1941; Criterion Collection, 2001). See also James Harvey, *Romantic Comedy in Hollywood, Lubitsch to Sturges* (New York: Knopf, 1987), 566–582.

2. Harvey, *Romantic Comedy in Hollywood*, 570–571.

3. See my book *Three Philosophical Filmmakers: Hitchcock, Welles, Renoir* (Cambridge, Mass.: The MIT Press, 2004), 82–87 and passim.

4. See Stanley Cavell, *Pursuits of Happiness: The Hollywood Comedy of Remarriage* (Cambridge, Mass.: Harvard University Press, 1981), 45–70, as well as "*The Lady Eve*," in his *City of Words: Pedagogical Letters on a Register of the Moral Life* (Cambridge, Mass.: Harvard University Press, 2004), 301–312. See also Marian Keane, audio commentary in *The Lady Eve*, DVD, directed by Preston Sturges (1941; Criterion Collection, 2001), which contains many suggestive insights.

5. On mirrors and the photographic image, see my book *Reality Transformed: Film as Meaning and Technique* (Cambridge, Mass.: The MIT Press, 1998), 92–95.

6. On this, see Charles Musser, "Divorce, DeMille and the Comedy of Remarriage," in *Classical Hollywood Comedy*, ed. Kristine Brunovska Karnick and Henry Jenkins (New York: Routledge, 1995), 282–313, particularly 283–285.

7. See my book *Ingmar Bergman, Cinematic Philosopher: Reflections on His Creativity* (Cambridge, Mass.: The MIT Press, 2007), 4.

8. At this point Martin Marks made these comments in a personal letter, for which I am very grateful, about the music in the train sequence:

First, at the start of the conversation, before things heat up, there is a soft cello cello, which sounds to me like a subtle reference to music from the prelude to the opening scene of Act IV of Verdi's *Don Carlos*. This is the scene of King Phillip's magnificent "Elle ne m'aime pas," that is, "She [the queen] doesn't love me." Could the music director of the film have been making a coy reference? I cannot tell you.

The next passage, though, is clearly the music of Wagner's Pilgrim's Chorus from *Tannhäuser*. This enters at the point where Charles begins to offer his "sweet forgiveness" to Eve. That allusion is of course a mocking one — much like the way Sturges used the piece, far more extensively, as the second classical work featured in the masterpiece *Unfaithfully Yours*, for the scenario in which Rex Harrison (Sir Alfred) forgives Linda Darnell (Daphne).

Finally, at Fonda's bemused response to Eve, "*Herman?*," the third piece begins. It is an excerpt from the middle of Franz von Suppé's "Poet and Peasant Overture," which introduced his opera *Dichter und Bauer* (a "lustspiel" in three acts), first performed in 1846. The overture became a concert favorite and was much played during silent film days by orchestras accompanying films with composite scores. The stormy music only lasts for a minute or two, within an overture of about ten and a half minutes.

By the way, the Internet Movie Database (imdb.com) has a "Soundtrack" link on the *Lady Eve* page which supposedly lists the pieces heard in the film. That list does not have the von Suppé and mistakenly identifies the music as being from Rossini's *Barber of Seville*. But this attribution is incorrect, as you know.

2 Pygmalion Variations

1. *The Metamorphoses of Ovid,* trans. freely into verse by David R. Slavitt (Baltimore, Md.: The Johns Hopkins University Press, 1994), 202.

2. Bernard Shaw, *Pygmalion: A Romance in Five Acts* (London: Penguin, 2000), 148.

3. Quoted in an appendix in Donald P. Costello, *The Serpent's Eye: Shaw and the Cinema* (Notre Dame, Ind.: Notre Dame University Press, 1965), 188.

4. Quoted in Costello, *The Serpent's Eye,* 68.

5. Quoted in Costello, *The Serpent's Eye,* 9.

6. Quoted in Costello, *The Serpent's Eye,* 146.

7. Bernard Shaw, *Pygmalion: A Romance in Five Acts,* 63.

8. Bernard Shaw, *Pygmalion: A Romance in Five Acts,* 133.

9. Bernard Shaw, *Man and Superman: A Comedy and a Philosophy,* in *Complete Plays with Prefaces* (New York: Dodd, Mead, 1962), 3: 746. On Shaw's thinking in *Man and Superman,* as well as other writings, see my book *The Nature of Love: The Modern World* (Chicago: The University of Chicago Press, 1987), 239–253.

10. Quoted in Bernard F. Dukore, *The Collected Screenplays of Bernard Shaw* (Athens: The University of Georgia Press, 1980), 226.

11. On this, see my book *Three Philosophical Filmmakers,* 28–33 and passim.

12. Quoted in Archibald Henderson, *George Bernard Shaw: Man of the Century* (New York: Appleton-Century-Crofts, 1956), 616.

13. For further discussion of *Pygmalion* in relation to the Cinderella myth, see Charles A. Berst, *Pygmalion: Shaw's Spin on Myth and Cinderella* (New York: Twayne, 1995). On related material, see also Errol Durbach, "*Pygmalion*: Myth and Anti-Myth in the Plays of Ibsen and

Shaw," in *George Bernard Shaw's* Pygmalion, ed. Harold Bloom (New York: Chelsea House, 1988), 87–98.

3 *The Heiress* and *Washington Square*

1. Henry James, *Washington Square* (New York: Signet, 1979), 221–222.

2. James, *Washington Square*, 5.

3. James, *Washington Square*, 5.

4. See Millicent Bell, *Meaning in Henry James* (Cambridge: Harvard University Press, 1991), 65–79.

5. James, *Washington Square*, 47.

6. James, *Washington Square*, 66.

7. James, *Washington Square*, 62.

8. James, *Washington Square*, 75.

9. James, *Washington Square*, 76.

10. On this, see Ian F. A. Bell, *Washington Square: Styles of Money* (New York: Twayne, 1993).

11. James, *Washington Square*, 147.

12. James, *Washington Square*, 148.

13. James, *Washington Square*, 91.

14. James, *Washington Square*, 144.

15. Ruth and Augustus Goetz, *The Heiress* (New York: Dramatists Play Service, 1948), 112–113.

16. On the house in Wyler's film, see Harry Horner, "Designing 'The Heiress,'" *Hollywood Quarterly* 5, no. 1: 1–7.

17. James, *Washington Square*, 80.

4 Cocteau: The Mythological Poetry of Film

1. Jean Cocteau, *The Art of Cinema*, ed. André Bernard and Claude Gauteur, trans. Robin Buss (London: Marion Boyars, 1992), 38.

2. Cocteau, *The Art of Cinema*, 40.

3. Jean Cocteau, *Professional Secrets: An Autobiography of Jean Cocteau*, ed. Robert Phelps, trans. Richard Howard (New York: Farrar, Straus, & Giroux, 1970), 147.

4. Cocteau, *Professional Secrets*, 145.

5. Cocteau, *Professional Secrets*, 147.

6. Jean-Paul Sartre, "Autoportrait à 70 ans," *Le Nouvel Observateur* 55 (June 30–July 7, 1975), 76; my translation. Passage quoted in French and discussed in Lydia Crowson, *The Esthetic of Jean Cocteau* (Hanover, N.H.: The University Press of New England, 1978), 162.

7. Cocteau, *The Art of Cinema*, 46.

8. Cocteau, *The Art of Cinema*, 161.

9. For this and other details about the shooting of the film, see Jean Cocteau, *Beauty and the Beast: Diary of a Film*, trans. Ronald Duncan (New York: Dover, 1972).

10. BBC documentary, *Laurence Olivier: A Life*, 1982.

11. For Cocteau's indebtedness to Welles, see Sir Christopher Frayling's excellent commentary in *Beauty and the Beast*, DVD, directed by Jean Cocteau (1946; Criterion Collection, 2003).

12. See Frayling, commentary in *Beauty and the Beast*.

13. Bruno Bettelheim, *The Uses of Enchantment: The Meaning and Importance of Fairy Tales* (New York: Vintage, 1977), 303.

14. Philip Glass, introduction to his opera / film in *Beauty and the Beast*, DVD, directed by Jean Cocteau (1946; Criterion Collection, 2003).

15. Thornton Wilder, *Our Town* (New York: Avon Books, 1975), 139.

16. On *The Seventh Seal* and in general Bergman's development as a philosophic thinker, see also my book *Ingmar Bergman, Cinematic Philosopher.*

17. Quoted in Jean Béranger, "Meeting with Ingmar Bergman," in *Focus on* The Seventh Seal, ed. Birgitta Steene (Englewood Cliffs, N.J.: Prentice-Hall, 1972), 12. See also Edward Baron Turk, "The Film Adaptation of Cocteau's *Les Enfants terribles*," *Cinema Journal* 19, no. 2: 25–40.

18. For further discussion of the Orpheus myth in itself and in relation to the films of Cocteau, see *Reviewing Orpheus: Essays on the Cinema and Art of Jean Cocteau*, ed. Cornelia A. Tsakiridou (Lewisburg, Penn.: Bucknell University Press, 1997); Charles Segal, *Orpheus: The Myth of the Poet* (Baltimore, Md.: The Johns Hopkins University Press, 1989); Inez Hedges, "Truffaut and Cocteau: Representations of Orpheus," in her *Breaking the Frame: Film Language and the Experience of Limits* (Bloomington: Indiana University Press, 1991), 52–65; Linda C. Ehrlich, "Orpheus on Screen: Open and Closed Forms," in *Representing Religion in World Cinema: Filmmaking, Mythmaking, Culture Making*, ed. S. Brent Plate (New York: Palgrave Macmillan, 2003), 67–87.

5 Mythmaking in Kubrick and Fellini

1. Arthur C. Clarke, *2001: A Space Odyssey* (New York: New American Library, 1999), viii.

2. Kubrick interview in *The Making of Kubrick's 2001*, ed. Jerome Agel (New York: Signet, 1970), 328.

3. Eric Nordern, "*Playboy* Interview: Stanley Kubrick," in *Stanley Kubrick Interviews*, ed. Gene D. Phillips (Jackson: University Press of Mississippi, 2001), 49.

4. Nordern, "*Playboy* Interview: Stanley Kubrick," 49.

5. Nordern, "*Playboy* Interview: Stanley Kubrick," 49.

6. Nordern, "*Playboy* Interview: Stanley Kubrick," 51.

7. In John Simon, *Ingmar Bergman Directs* (New York: Harcourt Brace Jovanovich, 1972), 22.

8. Paquito del Bosco, *Federico Fellini's Autobiography*, documentary in *La Strada*, DVD, directed by Federico Fellini (1954; Criterion Collection, 2003).

9. Del Bosco, *Federico Fellini's Autobiography*, documentary in *La Strada*.

10. "Federico Fellini," in *Conversations with the Great Moviemakers of Hollywood's Golden Age at the American Film Institute*, ed. George Stevens Jr. (New York: Knopf, 2006), 632.

11. *Conversations with the Great Moviemakers of Hollywood's Golden Age*, 638.

12. *Conversations with the Great Moviemakers of Hollywood's Golden Age*, 635.

13. Tim Dirks, "*2001: A Space Odyssey* (1968)," www.filmsite.org/twot.html, 4.

14. Nordern, "*Playboy* Interview: Stanley Kubrick," 50.

15. Nordern, "*Playboy* Interview: Stanley Kubrick," 49. His italics.

16. Tim Dirks, "*Dr. Strangelove, Or: How I Learned to Stop Worrying And Love The Bomb* (1964)," www.filmsite.org/drst.html, 2–3.

17. *Eyes Wide Shut, A Screenplay by Stanley Kubrick and Frederic Raphael, and the Classic Novel that Inspired the Film, Dream Story by Arthur Schnitzler* (New York: Warner Books, 1999), 234.

18. *Eyes Wide Shut*, 235–236.

19. *Eyes Wide Shut*, 271.

20. *Eyes Wide Shut*, 271.

21. *Eyes Wide Shut*, 245.

22. On the mythological dimensions of Beethoven's *Fidelio*, see my book *Mozart and Beethoven: The Concept of Love in Their Operas*

(Baltimore, Md.: The Johns Hopkins University Press, 1977), 118–152 and passim.

23. *Eyes Wide Shut*, 281.

24. *Eyes Wide Shut*, 164–165.

25. For further discussion, see Karen D. Hoffman, "Where the Rainbow Ends: *Eyes Wide Shut*," in *The Philosophy of Stanley Kubrick*, ed. Jerold J. Abrams (Lexington: The University of Kentucky Press, 2007), 59–83. In the same volume, see also Jerold J. Abrams, "Nietzsche's Overman as Posthuman Star Child in *2001: A Space Odyssey*," 247–265. See also James Naremore, *On Kubrick* (London: The British Film Institute, 2007), 222–242.

Index

Abrams, Gerald J., 238
Adam and Eve, myth of, 13–15, 17–18, 21, 28, 29, 38, 39, 55–56, 128
Akerman, Chantal, 78
La Captive, 78
Alcestis, myth of, 168
Alekan, Henri, 145, 161
Apollo, myth of, 188–189, 192
Appraisal and bestowal, 5, 121–123
Apuleius, Lucius, 157
Argus, myth of, 32
Asquith, Anthony, 54
Ate, myth of, 112
Athena/Minerva (Greek/Roman goddess), 149, 179, 180, 196
Auden, W. H., 17
Auric, Georges, 166–167, 192

Beethoven, Ludwig van, 164, 216, 225, 237
Fidelio, 164, 166, 225
Ninth Symphony, 216
Bell, Ian F. A., 234
Bell, Millicent, 98, 234
Benny, Jack, 44
Béranger, Jean, 236
Bérard, Christian, 145
Bergman, Ingmar, 41, 79, 120, 173–175, 181, 203, 236
Faithless, 51
Persona, 79
Sawdust and Tinsel, 203
Seventh Seal, The, 173–175, 203
Smiles of a Summer Night, 120
Bergman, Ingrid, 20, 156
Bergson, Henri, 8–9, 231
Berlioz, Hector, 137
Les Troyens, 137
Bernstein, Leonard, 227
Candide, 227
Berst, Charles A., 233
Bettelheim, Bruno, 164, 235
Uses of Enchantment, The, 164
Bogart, Humphrey, 17
Bringing Up Baby, 23
Buñuel, Luis, 142
Un chien andalou, 142
Burgess, Anthony, 216

Camus, Marcel, 190–192
  Orfeu Negro, 190–193
Capra, Frank, 41
Carson, Johnny, 208
Casablanca, 17
Cavell, Stanley, 29, 34, 37, 45, 231
Chaplin, Charlie, 44
Cinderella, myth of, 79–82
City of Angels, 170
Clarke, Arthur C., 197, 236
Cocteau, Jean, 11, 139–193, 225, 235
  Blood of a Poet, The, 142–143, 149, 165, 169, 179, 182–183, 187
  on cinematic poetry, 139–144, 156–157
  on film as dream and hypnosis, 141
  L'Eternal retour, 176–178, 187
  La Belle et la Bête, 144–168, 181–182, 186, 224–225
  Les Enfants terribles, 180
  Les Parents terribles, 180–181
  on magic and the magical, 145–147, 159–162, 176
  on mythmaking, 139–140
  Orphée, 168–173, 175–176, 181, 183–184, 187–189, 191, 193, 195
  Testament of Orpheus, The, 149, 168, 169, 170, 171, 172, 175, 178, 179, 184, 185, 186, 187, 193
Coen, Joel, and Ethan Coen, 50
Copland, Aaron, 112–114, 127, 132
Corneille, Pierre, 162
Costello, Donald P., 60, 233
  Serpent's Eye: Shaw and the Cinema, The, 60
Crowson, Lydia, 235
Cruise, Tom, 222
Cupid and Psyche, myth of, 157–158

"Daisy," 217
Dalí, Salvador, 142
  Un chien andalou, 142
Dante Alighieri, 188
  Divina Commedia, 188
Darnell, Linda, 232
Day, Josette, 154
de Havilland, Olivia, 126
del Bosco, Paquito, 237
Dellanoy, Jean, 176–178
Demarest, William, 14
de Maupassant, Guy, 94
Dermit, Edouard, 190
de Rougement, Denis, 177
Descartes, René, 152–153
Diana (Greek goddess), 148, 156
Dido and Aeneas, myth of, 10, 136–137
Dirks, Tim, 219, 237
Disney production company, 144, 147, 149
  Beauty and the Beast, 144–145, 147, 149–150
  Fantasia, 144
    Sorcerer's Apprentice, The, 144

Don Juan, myth of, 10, 15, 73, 95–97, 107, 123, 124
Doré, Gustave, 160
Dr. Jekyll and Mr. Hyde, 158
Dreaming as related to myth and cinema, 4–6
Dukore, Bernard F., 233
Dunne, Irene, 41
Durbach, Errol, 233
Duvall, Shelley, 221

Ehrlich, Linda C., 236
Einstein, Albert, 82

Fellini, Federico, 11, 195, 200–207, 220
  Amarcord, 203, 220
  Clowns, The, 203
  8 ½, 201–202, 204
  Federico Fellini's Autobiography, 204
  Ginger and Fred, 207, 220
  Giulietta degli spiriti, 205–206
  Il Bidone, 202
  I Vitelloni, 202
  La Dolce Vita, 201, 220
  La Strada, 202
  Lo Sceicco bianco, 202
  Satyricon, 206, 220
Flying Dutchman, myth of the, 36, 169, 227–228
Fonda, Henry, 43, 232
Ford, John, 11–12, 163, 209
Forman, Miklos, 86
  Amadeus, 86
Frankenstein, 158
Frayling, Sir Christopher, 235
Freud, Sigmund, 3–4, 19, 122, 141, 198

Garbo, Greta, 154
Gide, André, 179
Giotto di Bondone, 81
Glass, Philip, 167, 235
  his "opera/film," 167
  interpretation of Cocteau's film, 167–168
Gluck, Christoph Willibald, 171
  Orphée et Eurydice, 171
Goethe, Johann Wolfgang von, 17
  Faust, 17
Goetz, Ruth, and Augustus, 84, 85, 110–111, 116, 117, 120, 121, 123, 125, 234
Goldwyn, Sam, 60
Gottfried von Strassburg, 176
Grant, Cary, 20, 23

Harrison, Rex, 232
Harvey, James, 22, 231
  Romantic Comedy in Hollywood, Lubitsch to Sturges, 22
Hawthorne, Nathaniel, 84, 94
Hedges, Inez, 236
Henderson, Archibald, 233
Hepburn, Audrey, 69, 70
Hepburn, Katharine, 41
Herrmann, Bernard, 79
Hiller, Wendy, 69, 71

Hitchcock, Alfred, 20, 33, 45, 75, 76, 120, 156
Notorious, 20
Vertigo, 75–79
Hoffman, Karen D., 238
Holinshed, Raphael, 161
Holland, Agnieszka, 83, 114–115, 118–124, 129–136, 138
Washington Square, 83, 114–138
Homer, 6, 195–196
Honegger, Arthur, 59, 64, 80
Horner, Harry, 234
Howard, Leslie, 54
Hunchback of Notre Dame, The, 158

Icarus, myth of, 201
"I'm singin' in the rain," 217
Isherwood, Christopher, 209
Goodbye to Berlin, 209

James, Henry, 12, 63, 83–86, 88, 90, 92–94, 96–102, 105, 108–111, 114–116, 119, 123–124, 127, 130, 131, 132, 135–137, 234
Golden Bowl, The, 92, 137
Portrait of a Lady, The, 92, 137
Turn of the Screw, The, 99, 109
Washington Square, 11, 83–138
Wings of the Dove, The, 92, 137
Judeo-Christian mythology, 50, 52
Jung, Carl, 3–4, 19

Kafka, Franz, 179
Trial, The, 179
Kallman, Chester, 17
Kant, Immanuel, 19
Keane, Marian, 29–30, 34, 45, 231
Keaton, Buster, 44
Kemble, Fanny, 84, 86–90, 92, 98, 100, 102, 106, 109–110, 116, 135
Kidman, Nicole, 222, 224
King, Stephen, 221
Shining, The, 221
King Kong, 158
Kosinski, Jerzy, 197
Being There, 197
Kubrick, Stanley, 11, 195–200, 207–210, 214, 216, 217, 219, 221, 222, 223, 224, 225, 226, 227, 228, 236, 237
Clockwork Orange, A, 215–216, 217
Dr. Strangelove or: How I Learned to Stop Worrying and Love the Bomb, 208, 210, 215, 218–220
Eyes Wide Shut, 221–229
Killer's Kiss, The, 215
Killing, The, 215
Lolita, 215–216
Paths of Glory, 215
Playboy interview, 198–200
Shining, The, 208, 221, 222
2001: A Space Odyssey, 195–200, 209–214, 216, 217, 220

Lake, Veronica, 25
Lamorisse, Albert, 185
Red Balloon, The, 185

Lerner, Alan Jay, and Frederick Lowe, 54
Les Trés Riches Heures du Duc de Berri, 161
Ligeti, Gyorgy, 222
Locke, John, 107
Love of persons, 155–157
Love of things, 155–157

Madame Leprince de Beaumont, Jeanne-Marie, 149, 155, 163
Marais, Jean, 154, 162, 163, 190
Marks, Martin, 32, 232
McCrea, Joel, 25
McDowell, Malcolm, 208
McMahon, Ed, 208
Méliès, Georges, 197
Melville, Jean-Pierre, 180
  Les Enfants terribles, 180
Mirrors in film, 29–33, 184–185
Mozart, Wolfgang Amadeus, 7, 27, 44, 86–87, 95
  Don Giovanni, 95
  Magic Flute, The, 87, 226–227
Musser, Charles, 232
Myth and mythmaking, 1–12, 63, 65–67, 84–85, 93, 139–140, 163, 164, 168, 188, 196, 197, 206, 209, 211, 213, 214, 220, 225, 227–229
  as related to music and opera, 6–7

Nabokov, Vladimir, 215
Naremore, James, 238
Nicholson, Jack, 208, 221
Nietzsche, Friedrich, 176, 187, 214
  concept of eternal recurrence, 176
Nordern, Eric, 236, 237

O Brother, Where Art Thou?, 50
Odysseus, myth of, 50, 195–196, 229
Olivier, Laurence, 161
  Henry V, 161
Ophüls, Max, 227
  La Ronde, 227
Orpheus, myth of, 168–193, 228
Ovid, 53, 56, 57, 58, 74, 82, 188–190, 192, 193, 195, 233
  Art of Love, The, 58
  Metamorphoses, The, 53, 233

Pallette, Eugene, 25
Pascal, Gabriel, 54, 59–60, 70
Peck, Gregory, 156
Perrault, Charles, 80, 160
Petronius, Gaius, 206
Phantom of the Opera, The, 158
Philippe, Gérard, 227
Plato, 2, 157
Poseidon (Greek god), 196
Proof, 138
Proust, Marcel, 38, 66, 78, 86, 179, 215
Puccini, Giacomo, 79
Pygmalion, myth of, 10, 53–82

Racine, Jean, 162
Reality Transformed: Film as Meaning and Technique, 83
Reed, Tracy, 219
Rembrandt, 160
Anatomy Lesson, The, 160
Renoir, Jean, 32, 139, 151
Rossini, Gioachino, 82, 232
Barber of Seville, The, 232
La Cenerentola, 82
"William Tell Overture, The," 208
Rota, Nino, 204

Santayana, George, 16
Sartre, Jean-Paul, 144, 235
Schnitzler, Arthur, 221, 223, 224, 225, 227, 228, 237
Dream Story, 221–228
Schopenhauer, Arthur, 72, 227
Scott, George C., 208
Segal, Charles, 236
Shakespeare, 40, 42, 68, 73, 161, 177, 191
Hamlet, 128
Henry V, 161
King Lear, 91
Midsummer Night's Dream, A, 91
Much Ado About Nothing, 68
Romeo and Juliet, 191
Shaw, George Bernard, 11, 53–62, 67–69, 71, 72–75, 77, 81, 82, 233
Arms and the Man, 59
How He Lied to Her Husband, 59
Man and Superman, 73–74
My Fair Lady, 54, 58, 74, 75, 76, 79
Pygmalion, 53–82, 195
Signoret, Simone, 227
Simon, John, 237
Singer, Naomi Mae, x
Slavitt, David R., 233
Stanwyck, Barbara, 13, 17, 29, 42, 43
Strauss, Johann, 211
"Blue Danube Waltz, The," 211
Strauss, Richard, 196
Thus Spake Zarathustra, 196, 213–214
Stravinsky, Igor, 17
Rake's Progress, The, 17
Sturges, Preston, 13, 16, 22, 25, 26, 27, 29, 33, 38–40, 42–47, 51, 82, 231, 232
Great McGinty, The, 39
Hail the Conquering Hero, 39
Lady Eve, The, 11, 13–52, 54, 120, 232
Palm Beach Story, The, 25, 38, 50, 82
Sullivan's Travels, 25, 39, 40, 44, 50, 51
Unfaithfully Yours, 51, 232

Tirso de Molina (Gabriel Téllez), 96–97
Tristan and Iseult, myth of, 10, 67, 176–179, 181

Turgenev, Ivan, 94
Turk, Edward Baron, 236

Ullmann, Liv, 51
Faithless, 51

Verdi, Giuseppe, 7, 24, 35, 79, 228, 232
Don Carlos, 232
Rigoletto, 228
von Suppé, Franz, 232
Dichter und Bauer, 232
"Poet and Peasant Overture," 232

Wagner, Richard, 34, 169, 227, 228, 232
Flying Dutchman, The, 169, 227–228
Ring of the Niebelungen, The, 170
Tannhäuser, 232
Wandering Jew, myth of the, 36, 227–228
Welles, Orson, 11–12, 28–29, 40, 41, 139, 162–163, 235
Citizen Kane, 41, 162
Wenders, Wim, 170
Wings of Desire, 170
Wilbur, Richard, 227
Wilde, Oscar, 27
Lady Windemere's Fan, 27
Picture of Dorian Gray, The, 158–159
Wilder, Thornton, 171, 235
Our Town, 171–172
Wyler, William, 32, 83, 85, 111, 114–120, 123, 124, 125, 127, 128, 130, 132, 133, 134, 137
Heiress, The, 11, 83–138

Zeffirelli, Franco, 28